D0468138

GOLF
CHARACTERS

GOLF
CHACTERS

CARICATURES BY JOHN IRELAND

TEXT BY CHRIS PLUMRIDGE

INTRODUCTION BY TONY JACKLIN

STANLEY PAUL

LONDON · SYDNEY · AUCKLAND · JOHANNESBURG

Stanley Paul and Co Ltd

An imprint of Century Hutchinson
Brookmount House, 62-65 Chandos Place,
Covent Garden, London WC2N 4NW
Century Hutchinson Australia (Pty) Ltd
20 Alfred Street, Milsons Point, Sydney 2061, Australia
Century Hutchinson New Zealand Limited
191 Archers Road, PO Box 40-086, Glenfield, Auckland 10
Century Hutchinson South Africa (Pty) Ltd
PO Box 337, Bergvlei 2012, South Africa

First published 1989
© Lennard Books 1989
ISBN 0 09 174047 9

British Library CIP Data is available

Made by Lennard Books
Musterlin House, Jordan Hill Road,
Oxford OX2 8DP

Editor Michael Leitch
Design by Pocknell & Co
Production Reynolds Clark Associates Ltd
Printed and Bound in Spain by Nerecan SA

CONTENTS

When I was asked to write the Introduction to this book my initial response was to utter those fateful words, 'Well, of course, in my day . . .' I managed to stop myself going any further because I suddenly realised that, having been a professional for more than 25 years, I was in danger of falling into the nostalgia trap which is a sure sign of getting old.

On the other hand, I know for sure that in my day we didn't have an artist with the talent of John Ireland for capturing the essence of a golfer's character. These portrayals (with one obvious exception!) bring out those aspects of people which we can all see but hardly ever actually notice.

The selection of any group of golfers is bound to provoke debate. Usually the discussion centres upon whether a player from one era was better than a player from another. In the same way that a golfer can only beat those that are around at the same time, so he or she can only be a character in his or her own time.

When I first came into professional golf, there were so-called characters everywhere. There was the gypsy band of caddies – rogues and vagabonds every one. One of them, I think he caddied for Max Faulkner, used to carry Max's bag *and* a sandwich-board stating the odds on the day's racing, a sort of mobile *Sporting Life*. Max himself was a larger-than-life character with his colourful clothes and his collection of putters, including the famous one he made himself from a piece of driftwood. Tommy Bolt was another legendary character with his fiery temper and club-throwing – he always threw the club ahead of him because it saved energy. There was dear old Harry Bradshaw who travelled everywhere with his clothes in a little plastic holdall and who swung at the ball like a man tending an allotment.

Names come to mind like Ky Laffoon, who used to punish his clubs by tying them to the back of his car as he drove between tournaments, or Joe Ezar who once scored a 64 having nominated his score on each hole beforehand, or the great gambler and hustler 'Titanic' Thompson who was good enough to be a professional but made a better living fleecing the pigeons. All these people have added much to the colour and folklore of golf.

There are, of course, a million stories in the game and perhaps nobody told them better than Henry Longhurst. My own favourite of his concerns the occasion he was playing at Walton Heath with Viscount Castlerosse, an eccentric Irish Lord and a character if ever there was one. The noble peer was having a terrible day and on the final hole, having failed to move his ball from thick heather, turned to his caddie and said: 'Pick that up, have the clubs destroyed and leave the course!' All of us who play will know exactly how he felt.

Maybe the day of the total eccentric is over, but there are still plenty of characters about even though, in professional golf, life has become much more serious simply because of the huge sums of money available.

John Ireland's drawings supported by Chris Plumridge's perceptive observations provide an acute insight into some of the best-known names in golf. Do I agree with their selection? That's a question I'm not prepared to answer, but in my day . . .

THE POWERHOUSES

Everybody loves Sandy Lyle. The affable giant with the God-given ability to strike a golf ball immense distances remains essentially the same decent fellow both on and off the course. There is a lackadaisical air about Lyle which is reflected in his shambling gait, his lack of clothes sense and his apparent lack of emotion. People, however, all have their natural pace and Lyle's is slow – you only have to study the speed of his swing to recognise that.

The clothes sense is a natural legacy: Lyle has a long back, very long arms and exceptionally short legs for such a tall man. It's an ideal combination for a golfer but, unfortunately, not so ideal for keeping trousers looking neat and fitting. The lack of emotion is a façade. Lyle's inner feelings on the course can be likened to a duck swimming serenely on the surface of a lake. It looks effortless but underneath the legs are pedalling like mad. In the 1985 Open on the final green, when his little chip ran up the slope and back again, and in the 1988 US Masters when his final tee shot found sand, those were occasions when we saw the legs break the surface.

Alexander Walter Barr Lyle was born in 1958 the son of Alex Lyle, the professional at Hawkstone Park Golf Club in Shropshire. At the age of three, young Sandy was featured in the national newspapers as an infant prodigy who could hit the ball all of 80 yards. Practising under the stern eye of his father, progress was rapid and Lyle was a scratch golfer at the age of 14. Two years later he became the youngest competitor in history to survive three rounds of the Open Championship.

Being marked for stardom hardly seemed to affect Lyle. He continued through the amateur ranks combining brilliance with maddening failure, a pattern that has dogged him throughout his golfing life. It is quite inexplicable that a few weeks after playing in that Open in 1974 he reached the final of the British Boys' Championship and was hammered 10 & 9. A few weeks before his Open win in 1985 he was heading for a score in the 90s in the Irish Open before he picked up and withdrew. Lyle himself cannot explain these swooping troughs in his fortunes, he simply shrugs his shoulders and says if he knew the answer he would do something about it.

There is increasing evidence that Lyle, now past his 30th birthday, has found a greater maturity and is developing his full potential. His play at the final hole in the 1988 US Masters showed cool courage in the face of crisis and his winning of the World Match-Play title after four appearances in the final showed stubborn belief in his own ability. Match-play has never been Lyle's favourite form of golf since he finds it uncharacteristic to apply the killer blow to another golfer. 'I would much rather kill a golf course,' he says.

Away from the course, the slow-moving man has a passion for things which move fast, chiefly motor-bikes. He has boundless patience with young children and often amuses them with some swift sketches. He will ask his fellow professionals back to his house at Wentworth for a cup of tea and a chat. Indeed, it is this very ordinariness which makes him so popular with everyone. Perhaps the final comment on Lyle's essential decency should come from his long-time caddie, Dave Musgrove. 'When I stay at his house at Wentworth, he brings me a cup of tea every morning. Just tiptoes in, milk and no sugar. That can't be bad, can it?'

It can't be bad for golf when someone like Sandy Lyle is carrying the banner.

SANDY LYLE

Perhaps the most revealing aspect of Jack Nicklaus's character is that he hates surprises. Turn up unexpectedly at the Nicklaus front door or lay on a surprise party and you're likely to receive a dose of the gamma rays from those piercing blue eyes and a pretty peremptory dismissal.

Nicklaus likes to be prepared and ready for whatever is ahead. Couple this with a burning desire to win and you have a formidable combination. Ally those attributes with massive physical strength and the keenest analytical golfing mind the game has ever seen and you have, well, you have Jack Nicklaus.

In the style of classic American success stories, Nicklaus had no right to become the dominant figure that he has. There was no caddie-shack upbringing, no hustling for dollars *à la* Trevino and no grinding through pre-qualifying. The Nicklaus family were country club comfortable with the breadwinner a prosperous pharmacist in Columbus, Ohio. Membership of the Scioto Country Club followed naturally, and at the age of ten Nicklaus fell under two great influences that were to set him on his single-minded path. In 1926 the great Bobby Jones had won the US Open title at Scioto and, with a final total of 13 major championships, stood supreme as the greatest player the game had ever seen. The other influence was the Scioto professional, Jack Grout, a keen student of the golf swing and the man who imbued the young Nicklaus with the fundamentals.

As his game progressed at an astonishing rate, so the challenge of Jones's record grew as a target to be beaten. It was quite logical to assume that if Nicklaus could win 14 major championships then he would be regarded as the best ever.

Having got off the mark by winning two US Amateur titles, Nicklaus turned professional at the end of 1961 and the following year made himself thoroughly unpopular. The undisputed king of the game at that time was Arnold Palmer and Nicklaus had the temerity to tie with him for the US Open and then win the play-off. The Army was fairly abusive in its response. The fat, crew-cut boy from Ohio was booed and heckled. Not once did Nicklaus let his feelings be known but simply continued to let his clubs provide the answers. By the time he was 26 he had won all four major championships at least once, so he set out to win them all again. After a lean spell at the end of the 1960s he re-emerged for the new decade with a new slim figure, a new haircut and started setting some new records. In 1973 he passed Jones's record. In 1980, when he had been re-building his swing, he won two more majors. In 1986, when he had been virtually written off as a spent force, he won his 20th major with his sixth US Masters title.

Nobody pays closer attention to details than Nicklaus. It was he who pioneered the approach of pacing courses and creating yardage charts. He calculated what score it would take to win and planned his game accordingly and now, in tandem with his growing course architecture interests, he can tell exactly how a golf ball will react off different strains of grasses.

Jack Nicklaus set out to establish himself as a legend. His playing record and the courses he has designed will leave an indelible mark on the game. Away from golf he immerses himself in his family's activities, plays a hard game of tennis, collects fine wines, a pastime at which he is an expert, and enjoys the company of those people whose offbeat view of life is, perhaps surprisingly, in harmony with his own.

JACK NICKLAUS

Back in the 1950s there was an American professional called Clayton Heafner who was good enough to play in a couple of Ryder Cup teams. Heafner was noted for his temper. At one tournament, he arrived at the reception desk and was encouraged to do better than he had done the previous year. Heafner snatched up his kit, turned on the receptionist and said: 'Your town stinks, your course stinks and your goddammed tournament stinks!' He drove off without even hitting a shot. Sam Snead said that Heafner was the most even-tempered man he had ever met because he was always angry.

Craig Stadler gives the impression of being even-tempered in the Heafner manner when he is on the golf course. There is no poker-face reaction to a missed shot from Stadler, the club is thumped back into the ground or tossed back at the caddie, the head drops in anguish and one can almost see the steam emanating from the ears. As the indignities pile up, Stadler adopts a more philosophical attitude, as if he knows that whatever the outcome of a shot, fate is going to be waiting ready to deliver the sand-filled sock to the base of the skull.

Like many players who are gifted with great talent, Stadler finds it hard to tolerate any shortcomings in his game. His public explosions are merely expressions of disgust with himself and show how deeply he cares about fulfilling his talent. Some players have the capacity to bottle up their emotions; Stadler is not one of them.

Unfortunately, he is also one of those players whose temperament is constantly being put to the test by the vagaries of the game. For example, on his first visit to Britain as a member of the 1975 US Walker Cup team,

Stadler played in the British Amateur Championship. His caddie was so incensed by his master's abuse during one match that he dropped the clubs mid-round and told Stadler to continue on his own. For example, on the 71st hole of the 1982 US Masters, which he eventually won after a play-off, he struck a perfect drive down the fairway only to find his ball had come to rest in an old divot mark. Then there was the short putt he missed on the second day of the 1985 Ryder Cup match which provided such a psychological boost to the Europeans. Finally, there was the infamous towel incident. In the 1987 San Diego Open, Stadler hit his ball into the woods under a tree and had knelt down to play a recovery shot. As the ground was muddy and damp, he had knelt on his golf towel to prevent his trousers becoming dirty. He signed and handed in his card for the round but the next day was disqualified for 'building a stance'. The decision, however ludicrous, had to stand and it destroyed Stadler's year.

Yet Stadler has borne all this misfortune with good grace and a wry smile. Off the course he is easy-going and quiet, reserved even, very much the family man with a wide range of interests from skiing to the stock market. He can converse intelligently and lucidly on many subjects, all of which belies the image of the overweight, six packs of beer man that the tabloids unkindly christened 'Super slob' after his opening 64 in the 1983 Open Championship. Certainly he is no sylph and he cultivates 'The Walrus' nickname for marketing purposes, but the tempestuous figure he presents on the course is a far cry from the gentle man off it.

His loss of form in 1988 was attributable to a bout of mononucleosis which sapped his strength.

CRAIG STADLER

In an age when professional golfers appear to be stamped out from some repetitive production line, the presence of Fuzzy Zoeller is like a breath of fresh air on an increasingly solemn scene. The man whose name sounds like a character from the Muppet Show owes his unusual soubriquet to the fact he was christened Frank Urban which therefore produced the initials F.U.Z.

Laid-back is the best way to describe Zoeller's approach to the game. He ambles down the fairway, quietly whistling a tune to himself, exchanges a remark with the spectators, hits the ball and then continues in the same unflappable way. He is one of the game's more powerful hitters but the pace of his swing reflects his carefree attitude, being slow and leisurely. The style is unorthodox with the hands being held extremely low at address and the heel of the club against the ball. Although the swing is slow, there is a whiplash crack through the ball and the flight is naturally right to left. The same gentle pace is applied to the shorter shots and putts, all of which gives the impression that Zoeller plays the game at half-speed.

He grew up on the edge of a golf course in the town of New Albany, Indiana and was soon out there playing even to the extent of being entered for his first tournament at the age of five. Other sports came into his life and, like so many other professional golfers, the choice narrowed to a straight fight between golf and baseball. Of course, the Indiana winters made both sports impossible at that time of year so the alternative was basketball. It was during a high-school game that Zoeller received the back injury that was to threaten his career.

Zoeller first caught the public eye in 1976 when he produced a 63 in the Quad Cities Open which contained eight consecutive birdies, thereby tieing the record held by Bob Goalby. It was typical of him that he had to be cajoled into the press interview afterwards; as he said, he was just having fun and thought the feat was nothing remarkable.

He won his first tournament in 1979 which qualified him for that year's US Masters. Not since Horton Smith won the first Masters in 1934 and Gene Sarazen won at his first attempt in 1935 had any other débutant taken the title. Zoeller approached the Masters' pressure with his usual relaxed attitude. He never led throughout the four rounds but three crucial lapses by the leader, Ed Sneed, put Zoeller in a tie for first place with Sneed and Tom Watson. Zoeller then birdied the second extra hole to win.

While it might be considered that Zoeller backed into that major championship victory, his second, in the 1984 US Open at Winged Foot, demonstrated that beneath that affable exterior lurked a steely competitor. He and Greg Norman had an enthralling battle over the final round with Norman playing in the group ahead of Zoeller. On the 72nd hole, Norman holed an outrageous putt across the green for a par four. Zoeller, waiting in the fairway to play his second shot, thought the putt was for a birdie which would win Norman the title. In an act of sportsmanship, Zoeller waved a towel in mock surrender. Moments later he realised he needed a par to tie, which he obtained and then easily won the play-off.

At the end of that year he had to have surgery on his damaged back but has subsequently come back to delight the crowds with his powerful play and friendly response to people. He is no instigator of the quick grip in the Trevino mould but he maintains his cheery nature both on and off the course. Above all, Fuzzy Zoeller appreciates that golf is a game, a pastime that should be enjoyed and, as he himself once said: 'It sure beats working.'

FUZZY ZOELLER

It has been said that every time a professional golfer pockets a cheque from the US Tour he should give five cents in the dollar to Arnold Palmer. Few people would argue with that as a means of acknowledging Palmer's enormous contribution not only to professional golf but to the game at large. Until the advent of Palmer in the later 1950s, golf was regarded as a somewhat genteel pastime and even though Snead and Hogan were in their prime, they never quite caught the public imagination. Palmer changed all that. Not for him the methodical, planned approach to a round of golf – instead the course was regarded as deadly foe to be battered into submission.

The son of a greenkeeper-pro from Pennsylvania, Palmer was raised on the virtues of hard work and simple requirements. His father, Deke, was a hard but fair taskmaster and instilled at an early age the principles that were to make Palmer a staunch defender of the game's traditions and responsibilities. Deke Palmer also gave his son the basis for perhaps the soundest grip on the club the game has ever seen and this, combined with a pair of stevedore arms and a lithe but sturdy frame, gave Palmer a head start.

The Palmer swing was never a thing of beauty, it simply reflected his barnstorming approach. It was an approach that the public could relate to and, with Palmer's arrival on the scene coinciding with televised golf, that particular medium could not have had a more inspirational messenger. Palmer went for shots that other players backed away from, he hit the ball with unabashed ferocity, often into inhospitable spots, and then recovered miraculously, and he holed putts fearlessly.

His deeds put golf on the map and the game surged in popularity. Prize-money increased dramatically and devoted followers of Palmer banded together to form 'Arnie's Army' and root for their leader.

As a principal keeper of the game's traditions,

Palmer realised the importance of the major championships and it was he who, almost single-handedly, revitalised the Open Championship in the early 1960s. He knew his place in history would not be assured unless he captured the oldest title, and although he failed by the narrowest of margins at his first attempt in 1960, he succeeded for the first time the following year. His game was ideally suited to British conditions because he was able, with his great strength, to punch the ball low under the wind and run it into the greens. His demolition of the field in the 1962 Open at Troon over a course made bare and dry by a prolonged drought, was perhaps the finest performance of his career.

His seven major championship titles were crammed into a seven-year period but this record does not reveal that the attitudes which carried him to victory were also responsible for some traumatic losses. Statisticians who pore over such records will point out that he never won the US PGA Championship and therefore cannot take a place in golf's Valhalla, but that is like saying that Bradman wasn't quite up to scratch because he only averaged 99 in Test matches.

Palmer's whole life has revolved around golf, and apart from piloting his own aircraft to and from tournaments he has few other interests. He loves to hold court among a group but is strangely reticent on a person-to-person basis. This is not surprising in a man who has been the centre of attraction for over 30 years. If he ever ran for President he would win in a landslide but politics do not interest Arnold Daniel Palmer, it's still the sweet sound of club on ball, the cries of 'Charge' and the scent of victory which spur him. Now, at the age of 60, he has to find his motivation on the Senior Tour, and while the hair may be receding in direct contrast to the waistline, the Army remains loyal to the man who virtually invented modern professional golf.

ARNOLD PALMER

Being in the right place at the right time is rarely achieved in the protracted drama of a golf tournament. The arena is so large and the play so spread out that the vital moment is often only witnessed by a handful of people. However, there are sometimes magnificent exceptions and there is not a golfer anywhere who, at the mention of the 1985 Ryder Cup, will not be able to conjure up a picture of Sam Torrance standing on the 18th green at The Belfry, arms aloft, tears streaming down his face, acknowledging that he had just won the decisive point in a memorable European victory.

It was a highly emotional moment for a highly emotional man who had just completed the perfect ending by holing a longish putt for a birdie before being engulfed by his team-mates and family.

There are no suppressed feelings in the Torrance make-up. When he is down it shows, when he is up it's clearly obvious. He is a man in love with golf, someone who enjoys the gruelling schedule that is the lot of a modern professional. In his younger days he used to play in every tournament as well as squeezing in as many pro-ams as he could. Now an older and wiser man he paces himself a little more but he still finds the joy of hitting a golf ball an intoxicating experience.

An only child, Torrance was born into the world of professional golf, his father, Bob, being a professional and much sought-after teacher. So, even before he turned professional at the age of 17, he was steeped in the game. His apprenticeship began at Sunningdale and it was here that he sharpened his gambling instincts in money matches with the other assistants, such contests being an integral part of life at the Berkshire club. From there Torrance moved on to Ham Manor in Sussex under the eye of Tommy Horton and began to play the odd tournament, but the distance between him and his father, his one and only teacher, was

too great so he returned home to his native Scotland.

Torrance's career developed in a strange pattern. For his first five years on the Tour he lay in the middle to lower echelons of the rankings and then in 1976 he suddenly upped and won two tournaments virtually one after the other. They were victories that even he cannot explain since he admits that he wasn't as controlled a striker as he became later. There were no other victories in Europe for another five years but his climb up the rankings was noticeable. There is no doubt that the breakthrough occurred in the 1980 Australian PGA Championship when he overcame an international field and boosted his confidence sky-high. The following season he took his first European title and has been winning steadily ever since.

He made his Ryder Cup début in 1981, losing to Lee Trevino in the singles, then in 1983 he struck the shot of the match when he pitched dead from heavy rough to earn a half with Tom Kite. He followed his 1985 heroics with another fine contribution in the historic 1987 victory at Muirfield Village. The possessor of a long, slow and rhythmic swing, Torrance is a long-hitter and excellent bunker player. With the inevitable pencil stuck behind his right ear he invariably appears to be enjoying himself while on the course. Off the course, he and John O'Leary have been known to send a ripple of apprehension through the ranks of the bookmaking fraternity and, one other word of warning, don't play Torrance for money at snooker – he's getting close to that century break.

An easy-going man with an off-beat sense of humour, he once mock-strangled a journalist in a pro-am after a bad shot, much to the consternation of the other amateurs. In fact, he is the ideal professional pro-am partner. Oh yes, and keep the Kleenex handy if Sam Torrance is watching an old 'weepie' on the television; that emotion is never very far from the surface.

SAM TORRANCE

Long-hitting has always held a special fascination among players. Those who are blessed with the ability to strike the ball a long way are watched with awe by those who are not. Of course, legends surrounding feats of prodigous distance all concern men – from the time of Edward Blackwell, who in the days of the guttie drove the 18th at St Andrews, through to the era of Sam Snead and Jimmy Thompson and then George Bayer, who without much doubt was the longest ever.

Women golfers have rarely entered into this particular aspect of the game, since any comparisons with men would be invidious. Babe Zaharais was reckoned to be as long as a good male amateur and caught the imagination with her simple explanation of her length: 'I just take off my girdle and bust it;' while Jo Anne Carner could hit them around the 300-yard mark.

Now there is Laura Davies. Not only is she without question the longest hitter the women's game has ever seen, she is up there among the longest men. Already the stories concerning her power are passing into folk-lore. There was the occasion when she defeated two former amateur champions in a long-driving contest with a blow of 282 yards over wet and soggy ground. Or at a tournament in Hawaii where, in more favourable conditions, she drove 340 yards and hit the 565-yard hole in two with a five-iron second shot.

Davies herself is a little tired of the constant references to her massive length. She is forever making the point that you don't win tournaments just by smashing the ball from the tee. She is quite right. Since she turned professional in 1985, the girl from West Byfleet has won all over the world. In her first and second years she topped the WPGA money list, winning the Ladies' British Open.

Then in 1987 she became the first British woman golfer to win the US Open. Winning on courses set up by the United States Golf Association requires more than just power, a player must be able to control all aspects of the game, particularly the short shots and the putting on greens which are usually lightning fast. Although Davies averaged 255 yards from the tee throughout that Championship, it was her short game which finally won the day.

Rather in the manner of Nancy Lopez ten years ago, the arrival of Davies on the women's scene has given the professional game on this side of the Atlantic a tremendous boost with prize-money spiralling up beyond £2 million. Davies means to have her share of that as well as a sizeable chunk of the dollars available in America. She is shrewd beyond her 26 years and having had a series of winter jobs as an amateur is well aware of the other side of the coin. She cannot herself pinpoint the reasons behind her astonishing ability since she has never analysed her swing nor had a lesson. She is a big girl with very broad shoulders and strong legs and she uses these to telling effect but she also has extremely sensitive hands and tremendous club control.

Linked to these physical attributes is an attitude which loves to take a risk. It's all or nothing with her – if there's a carry over water she'll never lay up short, she'll always go for it. Sometimes she'll balloon to double figures, but more often than not it's a birdie or an eagle.

The gambling instinct runs strong in Laura Davies' life. She likes to bet on the horses, owns a greyhound and is thoroughly at home in a casino with a game of blackjack. Not for her the nun-like existence of the early-to-bed-with-a-good-book brigade – this girl is going places and enjoying every minute along the way.

LAURA DAVIES

Power has played a key role in the life and times of Greg Norman. The tall, blond Australian with the looks and physique of a Bondi Beach life-guard is the longest and straightest hitter in the modern game and thus can reduce any course to a mere fraction of its intended length.

While Norman generates power on the golf course, he likes to be around machines which generate considerable power in their own right. He recently added another Ferrari to his collection of motoring exotica, this latest model being an F40 of which only 750 were built and cost over £200,000 each. The car is capable of over 200 mph and, although he would like to drive at this speed, he realises that this sort of car is more than simply an indulgence, it is a rapidly appreciating investment. His love of speed is also demonstrated by his close friendship with Nigel Mansell and he is a frequent attender in the pits at Grand Prix races.

It was the thrust of powerful engines which nearly lured Norman away from golf altogether. He only took up the game at the age of 16 after reluctantly caddying for his mother, a three-handicap player. Having excelled at all sports, he regarded golf as a cissy game and not in keeping with the macho Aussie image. Besides, he was all set to join the Royal Australian Air Force to train to become a fighter pilot. However, after a couple of swings with his mother's clubs he found there was a great deal more to golf than met the eye and he was hooked. His mother gave him two books by Jack Nicklaus and within two years he was down to scratch. It was then that he arrived at the recruiting office with his father to sign the papers which would commit him to a life in the RAAF. This would be the fulfillment of his boyhood dreams, but just as he was about to sign, he threw down the pen and declared he was going to be a professional golfer.

Golf had come easily to Norman and so did his first professional victory, in his fourth tournament. He was hailed as the new Nicklaus but he kept a clear perspective on his progress and did not rush into the lion's den of the US Tour until he had served his apprenticeship elsewhere. He arrived in Britain in 1977, winning a tournament in that year, and then over the next six years he amassed a host of titles before committing full-time to America in 1984.

Here his aggressive style of play came into its own and he won twice that year as well as tieing with Fuzzy Zoeller for the US Open. Then in 1986 he had a year that could have been sensational but ended up only magnificent. He led going into the final round in all four of the major championships but ended up by winning just one, the Open Championship at Turnberry. He topped the US Tour money list and won nine events world-wide. He was the golfer of the year but it was a year which cast a few seeds of self-doubt. In the US PGA he had thrown away a four-stroke lead with nine holes to play and was beaten when the eventual winner, Bob Tway, holed from a bunker on the 72nd green. As if this wasn't enough of a blow, in the next major championship, the 1987 US Masters, he was again cruelly robbed when Larry Mize holed from 30 yards to win on the second extra hole.

Not surprisingly, these two defeats took some of the steam out of Norman's performances although he bore them both with a smile. Only time will tell whether the mental scars inflicted have healed sufficiently. He is also perhaps the most highly visible of all current top players and has been marketed successfully and lucratively throughout the world. He lives in North Palm Beach, Florida where he enjoys tinkering with his cars, playing snooker and fishing, but not for sharks. His 'Great White Shark' title came about because he used to shoot at sharks with a rifle when fishing in Australia – because they ate his bait.

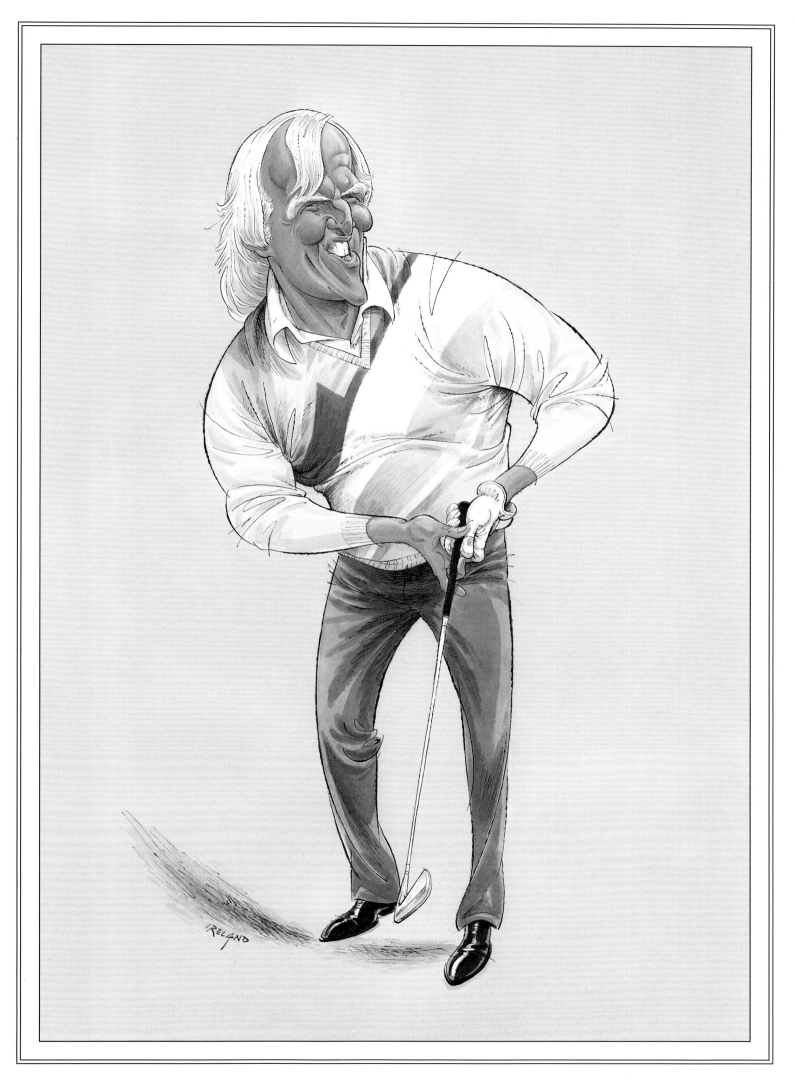

GREG NORMAN

The life of Samuel Jackson Snead is certainly stranger than fiction. He grew up around the Blue Ridge Mountains of Virginia, the son of a dirt farmer. His was a real hill-billy upbringing, shooting racoons and bear for the dinner table, acting as lookout for the moonshiners whose illicit stills were often raided by the revenue men. In those days of the Great Depression, it was a life of grinding poverty.

Snead took to caddying at a nearby course to earn a few nickels and dimes and then disappeared into the woods to cut down a maple tree branch which he fashioned into some sort of golf club. Copying his elder brother's baseball style, Snead developed a big roundhouse swing which generated tremendous power. It also helped that he was double-jointed and therefore could create great clubhead speed.

He was what was known as a 'peckerwood', and when he came down from the hills in the mid-1930s the hayseed was still in his hair. By now he had acquired a motley selection of clubs but it wasn't too long before the stories surrounding his prodigous hitting began to spread. An influential benefactor recognised this talent and got Snead a job as assistant professional at the nearby Greenbrier Hotel which was just about the classiest joint in the entire State. In his first week Snead was nearly fired. Playing behind one of the richest members he unleashed one of his rockets from the tee and the ball landed on the green 335 yards away. The member, whose company happened to own the hotel, thought Snead had hit his second shot before the green was clear. When Snead repeated the feat in front of him, one of the most remarkable careers in the professional game was launched.

It's a career which has spanned over 50 years. His contemporaries, at various times, have been Nelson and Hogan, Cotton and Locke and Palmer and Nicklaus. He is an amazing athlete, capable of kicking a 6ft 6in door lintel, and with a lazy, rhythmic swing which has stood the test of time he has compiled an astonishing record. He is credited with 84 official US Tour victories but his total is nearer 135 including regional events. He won seven major championships but never won the US Open, losing a play-off and coming close several other times. At the age of 62 he finished third in the US Masters and, when he reached his seventies, he beat his age so often it no longer caused a stir.

His total money winnings over 43 years came to less than $1 million and it has been calculated that at present values his winnings would approach $10 million. Talking about money was one of Snead's favourite subjects and he deliberately cultivated the legend surrounding his apparent meanness. It was said that he kept his cash in tomato soup cans buried in his back garden. He never denied it but years later when asked he replied: 'A damn lie, I never used tomato cans.'

Talking with Snead is always entertaining, a mixture of home-spun backwoods descriptions larded with profanity. Most of his stories are unrepeatable, either because they libel the living or they are just too crude. One of the stories that can be repeated concerns the occasion Snead came over to compete in the 1946 Open at St Andrews. Travelling on the train from Edinburgh to the ancient Burgh, Snead looked out of the window and remarked to his travelling companion that there seemed to be an old, abandoned golf course by the railway tracks. His companion, a dour old Scot, nearly had a coronary. 'That, Sir,' he spluttered, 'is the Old Course at St Andrews. It is not now, nor ever will be, abandoned.' Snead won that Open but never formed any great affection for world travel. 'Anytime you leave America,' he once said, 'you're just camping out.'

With his old coon dog by his side, Snead is never happier than when he's fishing in the mountain streams near his Virginia home. As someone once said, 'You can take the hill-billy out of the mountains but you can't take the mountains out of the hill-billy.'

SAM SNEAD

Welsh golf has a tradition of producing doughty fighters. The ebullience of Dai Rees and the tenacity of Brian Huggett are part of the Principality's heritage. In Ian Woosnam the country has unearthed another.

Woosnam simply oozes aggression. From his booming tee shots to his quick, swaggering walk the impression is one of bustling urgency and that nothing short of a cataclysmic explosion will halt his progress.

Harnessing that driving force has been the hardest battle that Woosnam has fought. Short of stature and pugnacious by nature, he is the epitome of the little guy who is prepared to take on all-comers. Even as a schoolboy he revealed this characteristic when, because of his lack of inches, he was picked on by the bigger boys. A few noses compressed on the end of a Woosnam fist soon put an end to that. Further evidence of his pugilistic abilities was provided when he entered a tiny tots boxing competition at a Butlin's holiday camp. One by one his opponents smacked their lips at the sight of their diminutive challenger and one by one they were helped from the ring with a fat lip as Woosnam went on to win the contest and a free holiday for the family.

Growing up on the family farm near Oswestry, Woosnam had none of the golfing advantages of his neighbour, Sandy Lyle, who, as the son of a professional, only had to walk out of the front door to be on the golf course. Instead, Woosnam pursued the farming life – lifting bales of straw, milking the cows, cleaning the cowshed and driving the tractor as soon as his feet could reach the pedals. It was a hard life but it meant that the youngster became immensely strong and extremely capable.

His father, Harold, introduced him to golf at the Llanymynech course which has the curious distinction of having some holes in Wales and some in England. Within six years of that introduction Woosnam had a handicap of one and was vying with Lyle for Shropshire county honours.

By now he had set his sights firmly on a career in the professional ranks and took the plunge at the age of 18. It was another hard row he had to hoe. Three times he attended the Tour qualifying school and his prize-money over the first five years amounted to a paltry £6,000. Blessed with his astonishing ability to hit the ball a long way, he still could not produce the scores. A healthy interest in the *après-golf* social life didn't help either.

It was a session on the practice ground prior to the 1982 Nigerian Open that changed Woosnam's ways. Here he watched Gordon J. Brand, the slow-swinging Yorkshireman, spraying balls to all four corners of the compass. At the end of day it was Brand who scored 68 while Woosnam had taken 77 and it taught him that perfection on every shot wasn't the requirement, it was what went down on the card.

With the scales falling from his eyes, Woosnam started scoring. No more beer sessions with his mates, this was deadly serious. The first win came in 1982 and the rest, as they say, is history. Ryder Cup honours, World Cup victory for Wales, a host of tournament wins culminating in becoming the first man to win £1 million in a season during his *annus mirabilis* of 1987, the year he also became the first British winner of the World Match-Play title by defeating his old rival Sandy Lyle in the final.

Now the trappings of success are plain to see. The expensive machinery parked outside the family home in Oswestry and the indulgence of a separate snooker room, complete with bar, sauna and jacuzzi. The rough edges of his background still remain with Ian Woosnam and he has yet to learn how to handle controversial issues diplomatically. Whether the problems are on or off the golf course he meets them head on. The little big man of European golf knows no other way.

IAN WOOSNAM

THE ARTISTS

Golf's social structure has never rated caddies near the top of the totem pole. It is therefore hard to comprehend the standing of someone who is a caddie's assistant. In the brutal poverty of Buenos Aires in between the wars any job was better than none and so Roberto de Vicenzo started out as a *lagunero* (pond boy) whose job it was to retrieve balls from lakes, ditches and other inhospitable spots, leaving the caddie to get on with his job of carrying the bag and massaging his master's ego in the hope of a large tip.

Naturally the boy began to sneak off with a club and a few balls and started to build a swing. By the time he was 15 Vicenzo was spotted by visiting American professional Paul Runyan and advised to turn professional. Six years later he won the Argentine Open and PGA Championship, the first of more than 230 victories around the world. Nobody has won more.

While many of his victories were in his homeland, he was a player of international stature and admired and genuinely liked by all who crossed his path. A burly man of nearly 15 stone he greeted everybody affably and always had a word of encouragement for the younger players. Indeed it was Vicenzo who counselled the 22-year-old Severiano Ballesteros on how to tackle the Lytham St Annes links prior to the latter's victory there in 1979.

Vicenzo had an easy, graceful swing which dispatched the ball with great power. He first came to Britain in 1948 and finished third in the Open Championship. It was the beginning of a long-running saga which was to last nearly 20 years. In 1949 he was third again, in 1950 he was second and in 1956 third. In the 1960 Open he led the field with a pair of 67s but fell away. He had problems with his putting and in his broken English once said: 'I play good but on greens like a motor-cycle, putt, putt, putt, putt'. Throughout his career Vicenzo had been plagued by a hook which, for such a long hitter, was extremely destructive. Having come close to a couple more Opens in 1964 and 1965, he resolved to cure his problem. He weakened his left-hand grip and embarked on a regime of hitting a thousand balls a day for six months. He also developed a stiff-armed putting stroke to combat his failures near the hole.

The changes paid off and at Hoylake in 1967, under extreme pressure over the closing holes, he played quite magnificently to win the Open at last, and such was the affection for him there wasn't a soul on the course who begrudged him that moment.

Less than a year later he was the unwitting victim of a scorecard error in the US Masters. He had birdied the 17th hole in the final round but his marker put down a four instead of a three. Vicenzo completed the round in what was thought to be a 65 which would have tied Bob Goalby. He quickly checked his card and signed it as he was being hurried along by a frantic TV interviewer. He failed to notice the error and the higher score had to stand giving him a round of 66 and Goalby the title. His demeanour over the incident and his response 'What a stupid I am' gained him a million more admirers. It says much for his character that within two weeks he was victorious in the Houston Champions tournament.

Now very much an elder statesman, Vicenzo is still active on the US Senior Tour. He lives in Buenos Aires and is a keen fisherman and tennis player as well as a devotee of the national religion, soccer.

ROBERTO DE VICENZO

The notion that the Japanese are a nation of small people is somewhat belied by the presence of Isao Aoki. Standing at over six feet tall, the man who earned the nickname the 'Tokyo Tower' when he was a caddie at the Abiko Club in Chiba, has been the dominant Japanese professional for the past decade.

In the manner of all young caddies, Aoki spent countless hours chipping and putting during off-duty moments, developing the sensitive touch which is the cornerstone of his game. Also, in true caddie tradition, he was given a set of clubs, in this case by an American serviceman, but they were too long for the youngster so he learned to adapt to them. It was from this that he developed his curious round-house swing which apparently defies all the popular tenets regarding the fundamentals of a sound method. Even more odd is the putting style which has the toe of the club cocked up but any amusement this might cause is quickly tempered by the frequency with which the ball disappears into the hole.

Aoki turned professional in 1964 but it took him seven years to achieve any standing on the Japanese circuit. Thereafter his success was spectacular and his current total of victories is well over the 50 mark, making him a yen billionaire.

Like certain wines, Japanese golfers do not usually travel well on the occasions they venture overseas. Aoki has proved to be the exception. His peculiar whiplash swing and toe-up putting stroke caught the eye of the British public in the 1978 Open Championship at St Andrews when he tied for the 36-hole lead. Later that year he took a giant step towards establishing an international reputation when he captured the World Match-Play Championship title and the following year he put up a stout defence, losing to Bill Rogers in a wonderful match which went to the 36th hole.

Aoki came as close as any Japanese golfer to winning a major championship in the 1980 US Open at Baltusrol. Indeed his first three rounds of 68 each set a new 54-hole record for the event. Unfortunately, the record was also tied by a certain Jack Nicklaus and although Aoki battled gamely against the man with whom he had been paired for all four rounds of the Championship, his final round of 70 was not good enough against Nicklaus's 68. In the same year he tied Mark Hayes's record for the lowest round in the Open Championship when he produced a 63 at Muirfield.

Aoki's lone victory on the US Tour came in a remarkable finish to the 1983 Hawaiian Open. Playing the par-five finishing hole at the Waialae Country Club, he needed an eagle to win and a birdie to tie American Jack Renner. After two shots he was still 130 yards from the hole in the left-hand rough. Taking a pitching wedge he knocked the ball up towards the pin and the gallery roared as it dropped into the hole. It was the first and, to date, only victory on the US Tour by a Japanese player. Later that year, Aoki was also victorious in the European Open at Sunningdale.

Aoki's English is limited and when he travels he engages the services of an interpreter for interviews. On the other hand, he knows a great deal more English than he is prepared to reveal and has been known to play tricks on interpreters by answering a question in English and then listening with a huge smile on his face as the interpreter repeats the answer, also in English!

ISAO AOKI

The search for the perfect swing is a quest which has occupied golfers since early golfing man picked up a stick and took a swipe at a nearby pebble. One of its most ardent followers in recent times has been Thomas Sturges Watson whose keen, incisive mind coupled with a psychology degree from Stanford University made him one of the more likely candidates to discover that ultimate perfection.

Now in his 41st year, it is likely that Watson has secretly acknowledged that his goal is unattainable, but during his golden spell of Open Championship dominance he certainly had it in his sights on several occasions. Of course, the application of clubhead to ball in a perfect arc is utterly useless unless it is accompanied by a fierce desire for victory. In this respect Watson has few peers, but the blending of these two aspects of a champion golfer took some time to mix correctly.

When he first appeared on the professional scene he had an alarming propensity for frittering away substantial leads, most notably in the 1974 US Open, and was thus branded a 'choker' by the American press. Nothing could have been further from the truth for it was simply that his technique had not been refined enough.

Accepting the assistance of Byron Nelson, the former machine-man of American post-war golf, Watson was tuned and brought to the starting grid ready to fire on all cylinders. First, he shoved the 'choker' label back down the throats of those who created it by winning the 1975 Open Championship only after he birdied the 72nd hole to get into a play-off with Jack Newton. Then, two years later, he took on the undisputed king of the game, Jack Nicklaus, in head-on encounters and won them both. The 1977 US Masters found Watson and Nicklaus tussling for the lead until a Watson birdie on the 71st hole so stunned Nicklaus,

playing the 18th, that he dumped his second shot into a bunker.

What happened in July of that year, however, almost transcended belief as the two of them were locked again at Turnberry in the Open Championship. They matched each other shot for shot in a two-man contest, the rest of the field having been scattered in their wake, until Watson went ahead for the first time with a birdie on the 71st hole. In a grandstand finish he displayed nerve and resourcefulness in the face of a final green flourish from Nicklaus and notched up his second Open title.

Three more were to follow to bring him within one of Harry Vardon's record six victories as well as another Masters title and the US Open, a record which shows that he respects the vagaries of links golf, indeed positively revels in them. The Scots took him to their hearts and if a British player wasn't going to win the Open, then Watson was a very acceptable substitute. Freckle-faced and gap-toothed, Watson was likened to Huckleberry Finn when he first emerged but he was not prepared to allow any media hype into his life. There was to be no equivalent to Arnie's Army or the Golden Bear for Tom Watson. He shuns the limelight, is intensely suspicious of any intrusions into his family life, freely admits his Democratic leanings and plays the guitar to professional standards.

Tom Watson is very much his own man – he is also a very rich one, but money has never been the driving force in his life. Once, en route to an Open Championship, he stopped off at Ballybunion, that classic links course on the south-western tip of Ireland. The rain was lashing down and it was blowing a gale, but even after 18 sodden holes Watson was raring to go out for another round. Why? 'Because it's bloody good fun,' came the answer. That's someone who certainly has his priorities right.

TOM WATSON

A rope hanging from a tree in the back garden of his house in Johannesburg set the pattern for overcoming adversity that has so marked the life of Gary Player. Climbing that rope more times than his older brother, Ian, was an obsession for a small boy who was physically under-developed but had to prove that he was better than the bigger fellows.

The rope also served another purpose – it developed muscle. Thus equipped with an obsessive desire to win and a fanaticism for physical fitness, Player was ready to tackle the world.

From the narrow confines of South African golf his first venture abroad was to Britain in 1955. The British professionals were not impressed. Player had a grip more suited to strangling a mamba coupled with a steep, chopping swing. But he could get the ball round. A year later he returned and got the ball round Sunningdale in fewer blows than anyone else to win the Dunlop Tournament over five rounds.

He then took on the American Tour and became the running, weight-lifting, raisin-eating fanatic that everyone recognised. He wore black because he believed it absorbed the sun's rays. He sat at the feet of Ben Hogan and learned all he could about the swing. And he practised until he dropped. All of which brought its due reward. By 1965 he had become only the third man in history to have won all four of the major championships, the Open, the US Masters, the USPGA and the US Open.

It was in 1965 that he laid the foundation for his now-legendary recovery powers when he played Tony Lema in the semi-final of the World Match-Play Championship. Player was six down after 18 holes, lost the first hole after lunch and then set about performing the miracle. Gradually he whittled away Lema's lead, squared the match on the 36th hole and eventually won on the 37th. It was a triumph of sheer guts and willpower and encapsulated everything he believed in about life, his religious beliefs, his pilloried country. In short, it was the ultimate example of his 'I'll show them' attitude.

He continued to show them with two more Open Championship wins and two more US Masters, his last victory in the latter event in 1978 being probably the most remarkable of his remarkable career when he came from seven shots off the lead with a 64 to win.

So what makes Gary Player run? The world's most peripatetic golfer still commutes from South Africa to America where he is phenomenally successful on the US Senior Tour and yet he no longer needs the money. He will still fix you with those big, brown, staring eyes and declare that he is hitting the ball better than at any time in his life. He will tell the world that he owes all his victories to God and clean living, that he has visions of victory before they occur. Cynics will mutter that he is too sincere to be sincere, too good to be true, but, whatever people think, Gary Player is still the man they talk about and write about.

Certainly he is a complex character, full of contradictions, but perhaps the essence of Gary Player was summed up by a fellow professional who remarked: 'Oh, Gary just likes beating people.'

GARY PLAYER

'Seve sera el mejor golfista del mundo.' The prediction by Senora Carmen Ballesteros that her fourth son would be the greatest golfer in the world is now the reality. Wherever the dashing Spaniard plays, he is the man to beat and since he burst on the scene in the 1976 Open Championship he has brought a new dimension to the game.

Growing up on the north coast of Spain, the young Ballesteros had one priceless advantage – the family home was located on the edge of the Royal Pedrena golf course. The course was out of bounds to him but its lure drew the boy into caddying and gave him the appetite to play. He learnt his now legendary skills using just a single club and adjourning to the nearby beach; there he practised by hitting pebbles as real golf balls were not readily available. Chipping contests with his fellow caddies, for more pesetas than he could afford to lose, honed his short game and his competitive edge. With his three brothers already professionals, Ballesteros, S. turned professional in early 1974 at the age of 16. His début was inauspicious but by the middle of the following year word was filtering back that there was this young Spanish boy who really was something else.

The confirmation of that assessment was not long in coming. In 1976 he led the field after three rounds of the Open at Royal Birkdale with a brand of golf which found him in most parts of Lancashire. Not since the days of Arnold Palmer had somebody taken on a golf course with such fearless disregard. The crowds loved him. They gasped at his prodigious drives and watched in awe at his exquisite touch around the greens. A round with Ballesteros was a roller-coaster of excitement and drama.

Ballesteros did not win that Championship but it set him on his madcap dance of youth across the fairways of the world. He won in Britain, Europe, Africa, the Far East and, at the beginning of 1978, he won his first title in America. The victory was to sow the seeds of a stormy relationship with the US Tour Commissioner, Deane Beman, who, on the strength of that win, offered Ballesteros free entry onto the US Tour without going through the qualifying school. The offer was rejected. Ballesteros wanted to stay in Europe.

American golf did not take kindly to that snub and when Ballesteros won the Open at Royal Lytham & St Annes in 1979 in quite outrageous fashion, his detractors were quick to dub him as a 'slasher' and a 'car park champion' after his tee shot at the 16th in the final round finished under some vehicles.

Nothing motivates Ballesteros more than injured pride and he emerged in 1980 with a more controlled swing but with the flair still intact. He decimated the field in the 1980 US Masters at Augusta National but still resisted the siren call of commitment to the US Tour.

Certainly Ballesteros is uncompromising when he feels his pride is hurt. He fought authority over the appearance money issue in Europe, he continues to fight the US Tour and he nurses a brooding sense of revenge for anyone who he feels has slighted him.

There is no doubt his emergence as a world figure has influenced the tremendous resurgence of European golf fortunes. His presence caused the Ryder Cup to be opened to Continental players and he is now regarded as one of 'ours' by even the most bigoted British chauvinist.

Ballesteros's record in major championships does not begin to compare with that of Jack Nicklaus but Ballesteros takes more risks in one round than Nicklaus has done in a lifetime. The important thing in Ballesteros's mind is to win and to hell with the consequences. His play and general demeanour in 1988 showed that he had recoverd from his father's death two years earlier and his marriage to his childhood sweetheart thrust a new maturity on his attitudes. His stunning repeat Open victory at Lytham was just a foretaste of much more to come. The Ballesteros era will last beyond the millenium.

SEVERIANO BALLESTEROS

Indirectly, the British golf tourist has played a key role in the development of Spanish golfers. With the great boom in holiday golf in Spain during the 1970s came a demand for caddies. In order to cope with this demand, clubs took to educating youngsters in the requirements of cadding and from there it was but a short step for these caddies to start swinging a club and becoming involved in the game on a passionate basis. Golf was a way out of poverty and the caddie schools of Spain nurtured the likes of Manuel Pinero, Jose-Maria Canizares, the late Salvador Balbuena and, of course, the country's most famous *golfista*, Severiano Ballesteros.

Social and economic changes have altered the caddie-school system. A higher standard of living means that fathers prefer to put their sons into an education that will train them for a good job. The caddies have been replaced by trollies and golf carts and the boom is over as golfers have sought less crowded resorts. The question therefore was, where was the next great Spanish player coming from?

The answer has been provided by the Real Club of San Sebastian in Fuenterrabia, home of Jose-Maria Olazabal. There was no caddie background for Olazabal, but his upbringing was still fixed in the game since his father and grandfather were greenkeepers. Furthermore, his mother and grandmother worked in the clubhouse but no-one did much to encourage him in golf since they were all too busy working.

Living in a golfing environment was enough for the youngster and by the time he was five he was taken under the wing of the club professional and from then on he was doing something that he loved.

In 1983, word began to get around that Spain had discovered the natural successor to Ballesteros. Displaying all his fellow Spaniard's consummate skill around the greens, but lacking the same power in the long game, Olazabal began to carve up the amateur events. The Italian amateur titles fell to him as did the British Boys' Championship. The following year it was the British Amateur at the tender age of 18 and then in 1985 he completed an incomparable hat-trick by capturing the British Youths' Championship. There being no more amateur fields left to conquer, Olazabal joined the paid ranks and, in 1986, set new records for a first-year player in Europe. He won two tournaments, recorded a stroke average of 70.69 for 72 rounds and finished second on the money list behind an all-conquering Ballesteros.

The following year was not so successful; he had no victories, but Ryder Cup captain Tony Jacklin had enough faith in his ability to select him for the match at Muirfield Village where he teamed up to great effect with Ballesteros. As the victorious European team celebrated on the 18th green it was Olazabal who showed a puckish sense of humour by performing an impromptu flamenco on Jack Nicklaus's sacred turf.

Olazabal's maturity is quite astonishing for one so young. His 1988 season brought two further wins to his name and he also developed a knack of playing to the galleries. Away from the course he enjoys going to the cinema and is particularly fond of American basketball. He is especially close to his family, and in the wintertime he and his father go hunting for pigeon and pheasant.

The achievements of Ballesteros cast a monumental shadow over any other Spanish golfer's record. Olazabal has secured his own piece of the limelight. He eschews any comparison with his notable countryman but there is little doubt in most people's minds that he is the heir apparent.

JOSE-MARIA OLAZABAL

'He never said anything bad about anybody, never.' Severiano Ballesteros's opinion of Ben Crenshaw coincides with just about everybody else's as the soft-spoken Texan has gone through his career acquiring a host of admirers. A spontaneous and emotional man, Crenshaw is probably too much in love with golf for his own good.

Not for him the hard-nosed approach that the Open Championship or the Masters are simply a couple of weeks' work, he not only regards the major championships as something special, he reveres them. He is Honorary President of the Golf Book Collectors' Society and has read all the classic golf books, soaking up the history and the folk-lore en route. His dreams of joining the illustrious names of the past on the roll-calls of honour have, therefore, placed him under additional pressure when one of the big four championships comes round.

Crenshaw emerged from the amateur ranks in 1973 with just about the hottest credentials since Jack Nicklaus turned professional a decade earlier. He had dominated college golf and when he won his first tournament as a professional, it looked like he was going to do the same in the paid ranks. Crenshaw had a long, flippy-wristed swing and was a little wild off the tee but the confidence of youth coupled with the smoothest putting stroke yet seen enabled him to redeem any errors. He was now rubbing shoulders with those legends he had read about and when the legends said his swing was too long, too flippy-wristed, he listened. Gradually he shortened the swing in an effort to gain more control but the move was against his natural instincts and, more often than not, he was caught between the two.

There's a condition on Tour known as 'rabbit ears' and Crenshaw had it badly. He listened to so much *ad hoc* advice that he couldn't see the woods for the trees. On most courses he was so far in the trees that he said, in a moment of self-deprecating humour, he ought to wear a red coat in case he was shot at by hunters.

The potential remained unfulfilled. There were victories on the US Tour but the majors continued to elude him. He tied with David Graham for the 1979 US PGA Championship but lost the play-off, he was second in both the 1978 and 1979 Open Championships.

Perhaps the turning points in his career were when he came to terms with two things, first, that his marriage wasn't working. He discussed his problems freely and openly and, in early 1984, the divorce came through. Second, he returned to his original teacher, Harvey Penick, back in Austin, Texas and worked on restoring the swing. The old freedom returned and with the putter working its silky magic, Crenshaw finally took that major championship he so richly deserved – the 1984 US Masters.

It was an emotional moment for the man to whom tradition, and all it stands for, is all. Keeping faith with the true spirit of the game is his abiding passion. He is certainly no fan of the current trend towards building 'stadium'-type courses, he abhors golf carts and dislikes the over-commercialisation of the game.

Some people may regard these attitudes as unrealistic, eccentric even, but that is to fail to understand how deep Crenshaw's feelings go. It's a depth of feeling he expressed himself in one sentence: 'I do not think I could go on living unless I felt that one day I might win the Open Championship at St Andrews.'

He has another chance in 1990 and is worth a fiver on the nose if only for the fact that nice guys don't always finish last.

BEN CRENSHAW

Women's golf in general has had a pretty raw deal over the years. This is not altogether surprising since the game is a male-dominated pastime and, for many years, its practitioners were deeply suspicious of any incursions by the opposite sex.

Over the years, however, a few women golfers have been given the ackno wledgement their talent deserved. Joyce Wethered, the dominant figure during the 1920s, was regarded by Bobby Jones to be the best striker of a golf ball he had ever seen. Twenty years later, that supreme athlete Babe Zaharias brought a new dimension to the women's game with her power and lithesome grace. She was followed by the incomparable Mickey Wright who set new scoring standards on the American LPGA Tour.

Without doubt the most recent figure to exert enormous influence on women's golf is Nancy Lopez. The timing of her arrival in the professional ranks coincided with an increased awareness of the potential of the American circuit as corporations had greatly boosted the levels of prize-money. Lopez acted as the catalyst, the player who not only projected an attractive personality but could play the game to a new and exciting standard.

Lopez grew up in the town of Roswell, New Mexico which also happens to be the home town of the singer, John Denver. She was of Hispanic stock and her father, Domingo, who ran a car repair business, was an accomplished low-handicap golfer. Her mother also played and, like so many success stories in the game, it was the visits to the local golf course that led to the youngster becoming hooked. From the outset she had no difficulty in hitting the ball and under the guidance of her father her progress was meteoric. Four years after she hit her first shot, at the age of 12, she was the women's New Mexico amateur champion, her score of 75 beating competitors two or three times her age. She then won the US Junior title twice as well as a host of other junior and college events.

A professional career beckoned and in mid-1977 she took the plunge, finishing second in her first event, the Colgate European Open at Sunningdale. But it was her play in 1978 that really caught the imagination and brought the crowds flocking. She not only won nine events that year, she won five of them in a row, setting new money records in the process. The following year she was equally dominant with eight wins and even more money. Throughout all this she still maintained her smiling, bubbly persona which endeared her to everyone.

An emotional woman who wears her heart on her sleeve, she suffered a cruel loss when her mother died just before her first professional victory. Her first marriage failed and she certainly lost her form while the trauma of that break-up healed. Pundits put her slump in the early 1980s down to her highly unorthodox swing without remembering that it was this same swing which had won her so much previously. But Lopez was having to do her growing up in the full glare of the public spotlight and that is never easy.

Now in her early 30s Nancy Lopez is a fulfilled woman. She remarried, to an American baseball star, Ray Knight, and they have two daughters. Golf is no longer the driving force in her life and she and her husband take their children to watch each other compete in their respective sports. She is regarded as perhaps the most competitive of all the women on the LPGA Tour and she is highly likely to burst into tears with the emotion of another victory. That is all part of the Lopez openness, the girl who will still smile through the tears. Indeed, a Nancy with the laughing face.

NANCY LOPEZ

If you passed Neil Coles in the street you could be forgiven for thinking he was a member of the clergy on his way to church. If you passed him on the golf course, you might even think the same thing. The balding head, the tufts of hair at the side running down into long side-boards and the benign expression all combine to give the impression that here is a man at peace with the world.

Appearances can be deceptive. At his peak, Coles was one of the truest strikers of the ball in the game, a player who was deceptively powerful despite a somewhat unorthodox set-up and was a wizard from 100 yards in. But underneath that seemingly unruffled exterior, demons were at work. A deeply intense man, Coles felt the pain of a missed shot sharper than most and was highly susceptible to succumbing to the red mists of anger that all golfers recognise. An experience at an early age taught him a valuable lesson. Playing in a qualifying tournament his ball, on a short hole, plugged in the overhanging lip of a bunker. He was unable to recognise the futility of attempting a recovery and hit the ball further into the sand. Further attempts followed before something snapped and he lost count of the number of times he hit the ball. He learned thereafter to keep the lid on the steaming kettle of his temperament.

Coles came into golf in an age when professionals were very much golf club servants – labouring unobtrusively in the background. Coles was an exception. Not for him the servile path, he wanted to play tournaments, an unlikely ambition for a player who turned professional at the age of 16 with a handicap of 14. His father was a successful businessman who was able to subsidise his son while he worked on his game as an assistant at various clubs. Picking up ideas as he went along, Coles developed a technique which worked. It involved hooding the face of the club at address which caused the clubface to be shut at the top of the swing. He was able to redeem this through the ball due to an exceptionally fine pair of hands.

He won his first big tournament in 1961 at the age of 27, curiously enough in an event where the large 1.68 ball was compulsory. The victory was something of a watershed for he became a strong advocate of the bigger ball, realising that it created better players. Indeed, his vision of the future extended beyond the ramshackle tournament circuit which existed in those days and it was he, along with John Jacobs, Peter Alliss and Bernard Hunt, who became the chief movers behind establishing a separate division of the PGA for the tournament professionals.

After much acrimonious in-fighting that division became reality in 1975 and Coles was elected chairman of the Tournament Committee. His guidance over the ensuing years has played no small part in the expansion of European golf.

Neil Coles won 33 titles in his career, including the 1987 Senior British Open, played in eight Ryder Cup matches and was the first man to win over £200,000 in prize-money. He was certainly good enough to win the Open but would not have relished the razzamatazz which would have followed. A fear of flying prevented him from becoming a truly international player so he concentrated on the domestic scene and was hugely successful.

The hands that wield that trusty old sand-wedge to such deadly effect are also put to good use in the construction of model racing yachts, or the renovation of furniture or the drawing up of plans for the design of new golf courses, this latter area being the blueprint for his future. Whether on the golf course or at his drawing board, Neil Coles is very much the master craftsman.

NEIL COLES

Countless successful professionals have been persuaded to put their thoughts down on paper regarding swing technique and instruction. Doug Sanders was different. His book contained a complete chapter of instruction on the seduction of women.

Sanders himself would be the last to deny that his reputation as a ladies' man was not fully justified but he was also shrewd enough to allow any embellishments of his various escapades to go unchallenged. It all helped to develop his carefully cultivated image of a roistering playboy who liked to drink and gamble in the company of beautiful women and who only used golf as a source of income when funds ran low.

Sanders's career spanned two eras. He first came to prominence in 1956 when, as an amateur, he won the Canadian Open. This was a grey time for golf with Hogan presenting an efficient but drab image for the game. The emergence of Palmer provided a much-needed boost and suddenly prize-money leapt dramatically. Sanders meant to cut himself a fair slice of that action and to establish his own personality on the Tour and with the public.

He had two things going for him. The first was his extraordinary swing which was so short that it was said he could swing in a telephone booth. Certainly the hands never went above hip-height and the club never reached anywhere near the horizontal, and with an extra-wide stance Sanders would flail through the ball taking care that the right hand did not cross over the left until the ball was well on its way. The swing had evolved from his youth when economic needs made the loss of a golf ball on the course in his home town a financial disaster of some magnitude.

The second thing was his wardrobe. Walter Hagen had been the first professional to dress up for golf and, after World War II, Jimmy Demaret had introduced the pastel shades that are so familiar now. It was Sanders who took over from Demaret and set new standards. He co-ordinated his outfits so that everything matched – shirt, sweater, trousers, shoes and socks, even underpants, all blended into a vision of yellow or red or magenta, depending on which outfit took his fancy on the day. In selecting his colour schemes, Sanders would visit a pharmacy and look through the different colour combinations of pills for ideas. His outfits caused such a stir that at one tournament the newspaper headlines ran: 'We don't care what Sanders shot, what is he wearing tomorrow?'

Good enough to win 20 times on the US Tour, Sanders was destined to become a nearly man in the major championships. He was runner-up in the 1959 US PGA Championship, the 1961 US Open and the 1966 Open Championship, but his most poignant loss came in the 1970 Open Championship at St Andrews when he missed a putt from less than a yard to win and then lost the play-off to Jack Nicklaus. The constant thumping into the ground with that abbreviated swing finally took its toll on Sanders's body and in later years he suffered from hand and shoulder problems.

A man from a poor background, Doug Sanders mixed with paupers and Presidents and treated them both the same. A latter-day Hagen who liked to stop and smell the flowers along the way, he had an acute golfing brain and was one of the best players in a wind the game has ever seen. A little like the comedian who wants to play Hamlet, Sanders would now like to be remembered for his work for charity and the world-wide junior tournament he administers each year rather than for his exploits as a country club Casanova. What he *will* be remembered for is that missed putt on the final green at St Andrews which made him one of the few exceptions to the rule that nobody remembers who finished second.

DOUG SANDERS

They don't make them like Lee Trevino anymore. Born on the wrong side of the tracks and a Mexican-American to boot, Trevino had to fight prejudice and poverty before he even put his big toe in the water of American professional golf. Yet this background was crucial to his success and provided golf with a classic rags-to-riches story which no Hollywood producer would entertain as being anywhere close to reality.

The Trevino legend has been well chronicled. How he hustled bets on a par-three course in Dallas by challenging opponents to take him on when he used an empty fruit-juice bottle, the opponents not realising that Trevino had practised for hours with the implement. How he used to play for more money than he actually had in his pocket and how, perhaps most importantly, he realised that winning at golf is not about developing a classic style, it's about getting the ball in the hole in fewer strokes than the other guy. Gradually, Trevino created a swing which would do just that, and although it was an ungainly thing his wife had enough faith in it to splurge her savings on entering her husband for the 1967 US Open at Baltusrol. Trevino finished fifth.

From that moment his fortunes soared and in the 1968 US Open at Oak Hill all the world heard of Lee Buck Trevino as he put together four rounds in the 60s to win. Now the Trevino that everyone recognises began to emerge. The poor boy who resented the world was replaced by the wise-cracking, smiling prankster of the links. A constant stream of jokes and chatter preceded each shot and the galleries loved it. His fellow professionals were not so complimentary. Tony Jacklin once told Trevino that he was not going to talk during a round. 'You don't have to talk,' said the ebullient Trevino, 'just listen.' Jack Nicklaus was diplomatic about the incident prior to the play-off for the 1971 US Open when Trevino produced a rubber snake on the 1st tee but was beaten, if not bitten, at the end of the day.

Indeed, no-one could keep Trevino down during a heady three-week spell in 1971 when he won the Canadian Open, the US Open and the Open Championship. The pundits who had scoffed at his swing changed their minds as Trevino showed his mastery over British links courses, flighting the ball under the wind and producing neat little chip and run shots. Here was a unique player who was a breath of fresh air on a somewhat dour professional scene and the British crowds loved him for his audacity and for his success.

Their devotion was a little stretched in 1972 when he snatched the Open title away from Jacklin, riding some outrageous luck en route to victory, but Trevino's own luck nearly ran out in the most final way in 1975 when he was struck by lightning during the Western Open. He survived but has suffered from back trouble ever since, undergoing a number of operations.

Some imprudent business dealings followed and he lost most of the fortune he had accumulated so he promptly set out to accumulate another. He divorced his first wife, Claudia, and married again to another Claudia – 'I married her so I didn't have to change the monogrammed towels in the bathroom' was his typical quip.

That there are at least two sides to Lee Trevino there is no doubt. On the course he is the joker in the pack but once the last putt is holed, the public persona vanishes. You don't see him drinking in the bar after a round and you rarely see him eating in a restaurant. Trevino quite simply disappears. Maintaining the 'Merry Mex' profile every waking minute is too much of a strain even for the man who created it.

Changing social conditions mean that the Lee Trevino story is unlikely to be repeated now that riches-to-riches has replaced rags-to-riches on the US Tour. He stands as probably the last graduate from the school of hard knocks and certainly will go down as one of its sharpest students.

LEE TREVINO

The 'Melbourne Tiger', as he was known, Peter Thomson was the greatest small ball player since World War II and compiled a record which warrants the title 'Best Australian Golfer of All Time'.

In the 1950s it was the Commonwealth twins of Thomson and Bobby Locke who held sway in Britain, in an age before courses were overwhelmed by raw power and skill and control were the chief factors. Thomson took a course apart like a surgeon performing an intricate operation. He plotted his way round, determining the best spots to be from the tee, where the trouble on each hole was located: he had no particular strengths and very few weaknesses. He accepted the vagaries of bounce and roll which inevitably occurred on fast-running links courses and turned them to his advantage. The result was an incomparable record in the Open Championship, five victories in all, three of them consecutively.

And yet the feeling persists that Thomson somehow earned his place in the game's history purely by filling a vacancy. In the period between Hogan's Open win in 1953 and the arrival of Palmer in 1960, Americans of any note just didn't make the trip across. Since America represented the best in golf, then Thomson was winning against the second-best. Furthermore when Thomson had taken on the Americans on their home soil, he hadn't exactly cleaned up.

The truth is that Thomson didn't fit into the popular conception of a professional golfer. He was a loner who disliked the pomp and glitter which surrounded American golf. He was intelligent, articulate and politically aware. He kept golf in perspective, once commenting on the futility of hitting a small white ball when thousands were being slaughtered in the killing fields of Vietnam. Here was a man who preferred listening to Mahler to post-round post-mortems, a man who could visualise a world tour from January to December, who could design a course and then write a sharp, perceptive piece for a newspaper or magazine, who stood for a seat in the Australian Senate and then began playing golf again on the US Senior Tour. Any doubts concerning Thomson's right to be judged among the all-time greats have now been dispelled as he took on the Americans on the Senior Tour and, in 1985, finished the leading money-winner with nine victories. So much for those critics who said he couldn't play on the lush grasses of the United States with the large ball.

Thomson was, and still is, a traditionalist. He hates the artificial watering of Britain's great links courses, he abhors the use of yardage charts and dislikes the hit-and-stick form of the game. His approach was entirely logical. You found a simple way of hitting the ball, you then hit the ball where you wanted it to go, you kept calm if something went wrong and you used your common sense.

Events have now overtaken Thomson's idealistic campaign and the race is now to the most powerful. His last defiant stand against the inevitable occurred in the 1965 Open when he won his fifth title against the entire might of the US Tour. He had other opportunities thereafter but a lively, inquiring mind and a desire to pursue other avenues removed him from the mainstream. Now aged 60 he is heavily committed to golf-course design and architecture but he could just as easily return to politics. Nobody knows which way this tiger may spring.

PETER THOMSON

In this age of burgeoning youthful talent it is not surprising to hear of 14-year-old prodigies producing scores around the level-par mark or grizzled veterans of 16 destroying the reputations of older, more experienced players. In the light of this trend, it is all the more revealing that Nick Faldo only took up golf at the age of 14 when he saw Jack Nicklaus on television and thought the game didn't look too difficult.

Such is the confidence of youth but in Faldo's case there was perhaps some justification since he was already an outstanding athlete in his chosen sports of swimming and cycling. Tall and broad-shouldered, he had the ideal physical build for these endeavours. At golf, however, above-average height can be a definite handicap. Certainly, he found the game much more difficult at the outset but his natural aptitude was soon spotted by Ian Connelly, the professional at the local course in Welwyn Garden City.

What Connelly spotted in that raw talent was an ingredient that cannot be imparted by mere instruction. It was rhythm, the pace of a golfer's swing which in nine cases out of ten can never be too slow. The cadence of Faldo's swing was a lilt, he didn't hit *at* the ball, he swung through it as though it were not there. When he attracted the limelight by winning the English Amateur Championship in 1975 at the age of 18, a leading golf magazine featured Faldo as its cover story. 'Do-ray-me-Faldo – Nick's swing hits all the right notes' ran the headline.

On turning professional, success was almost immediate for the big, rangy Hertfordshire lad. Selection for the Ryder Cup in only his second year in the paid ranks and a singles victory over Tom Watson thrust him to the forefront of attention. He was hailed as the new British hope and the player most likely to end the overseas domination of the Open Championship. His handling of the classic links courses of Royal Birkdale and Royal St George's, where he won two of his three PGA titles, also lent weight to that argument. He followed in the footsteps of Tony Jacklin, the last British player to win the Open, and embarked on a concerted attack on the US Tour.

It was clear that here was a man who was not content to settle for anything less than the best. His attention to detail, his relentless practising and his sheer single-mindedness set him apart from most of his countrymen. He believed in not sharing a hotel room since he didn't want his sleeping habits interrupted by someone else, he didn't spend time in the bar with the other lads after a round. All this dedication contributed to an image of a loner who was totally self-interested.

To a certain extent, these characteristics are necessary if a player is to reach the top but, of course, there are degrees. Faldo was winning tournaments, as in 1983 when he won five and topped the money list, but he was not winning friends. His first marriage disintegrated at the end of that year and his hounding by the tabloid press turned him against all representatives of that calling. In 1984 he challenged for three of the four major titles but blew up in one round in all of them. He knew it was time for a change.

A chance meeting with Zimbabwe-born David Leadbetter put the Faldo swing into a new slot but it took him two years to perfect it. During that time he ignored the doubters and pursued his new method with that same single-minded attitude. His reward came in 1987 when he did win the Open, firing a final round of 18 consecutive pars in vile weather; since then he has won the US Masters and become the most consistent striker in the world.

Controversy has dogged Faldo throughout his career. He drew attention when Sandy Lyle inadvertently broke the rules, he was the unwitting beneficiary of a mystery hand or foot sending a ball back onto the green during a match at Wentworth and, more recently, he was booed and jeered by Scottish students for refusing to play on in a fog-bound match at St Andrews. As one European Tour official put it: 'Nick has the unfortunate knack of being in the wrong place at precisely the wrong time.'

So is Nick Faldo misunderstood? It is more likely that he is not understood well enough since he has distanced himself deliberately from the mainstream of Tour life in his quest for success. Now he has achieved it and also become a devoted father to his new family, there are signs that a closer relationship between Faldo and the public is very much on the cards.

PETER THOMSON

THE PAR MACHINES

In this age of burgeoning youthful talent it is not surprising to hear of 14-year-old prodigies producing scores around the level-par mark or grizzled veterans of 16 destroying the reputations of older, more experienced players. In the light of this trend, it is all the more revealing that Nick Faldo only took up golf at the age of 14 when he saw Jack Nicklaus on television and thought the game didn't look too difficult.

Such is the confidence of youth but in Faldo's case there was perhaps some justification since he was already an outstanding athlete in his chosen sports of swimming and cycling. Tall and broad-shouldered, he had the ideal physical build for these endeavours. At golf, however, above-average height can be a definite handicap. Certainly, he found the game much more difficult at the outset but his natural aptitude was soon spotted by Ian Connelly, the professional at the local course in Welwyn Garden City.

What Connelly spotted in that raw talent was an ingredient that cannot be imparted by mere instruction. It was rhythm, the pace of a golfer's swing which in nine cases out of ten can never be too slow. The cadence of Faldo's swing was a lilt, he didn't hit *at* the ball, he swung through it as though it were not there. When he attracted the limelight by winning the English Amateur Championship in 1975 at the age of 18, a leading golf magazine featured Faldo as its cover story. 'Do-ray-me-Faldo – Nick's swing hits all the right notes' ran the headline.

On turning professional, success was almost immediate for the big, rangy Hertfordshire lad. Selection for the Ryder Cup in only his second year in the paid ranks and a singles victory over Tom Watson thrust him to the forefront of attention. He was hailed as the new British hope and the player most likely to end the overseas domination of the Open Championship. His handling of the classic links courses of Royal Birkdale and Royal St George's, where he won two of his three PGA titles, also lent weight to that argument. He followed in the footsteps of Tony Jacklin, the last British player to win the Open, and embarked on a concerted attack on the US Tour.

It was clear that here was a man who was not content to settle for anything less than the best. His attention to detail, his relentless practising and his sheer single-mindedness set him apart from most of his countrymen. He believed in not sharing a hotel room since he didn't want his sleeping habits interrupted by someone else, he didn't spend time in the bar with the other lads after a round. All this dedication contributed to an image of a loner who was totally self-interested.

To a certain extent, these characteristics are necessary if a player is to reach the top but, of course, there are degrees. Faldo was winning tournaments, as in 1983 when he won five and topped the money list, but he was not winning friends. His first marriage disintegrated at the end of that year and his hounding by the tabloid press turned him against all representatives of that calling. In 1984 he challenged for three of the four major titles but blew up in one round in all of them. He knew it was time for a change.

A chance meeting with Zimbabwe-born David Leadbetter put the Faldo swing into a new slot but it took him two years to perfect it. During that time he ignored the doubters and pursued his new method with that same single-minded attitude. His reward came in 1987 when he did win the Open, firing a final round of 18 consecutive pars in vile weather; since then he has won the US Masters and become the most consistent striker in the world.

Controversy has dogged Faldo throughout his career. He drew attention when Sandy Lyle inadvertently broke the rules, he was the unwitting beneficiary of a mystery hand or foot sending a ball back onto the green during a match at Wentworth and, more recently, he was booed and jeered by Scottish students for refusing to play on in a fog-bound match at St Andrews. As one European Tour official put it: 'Nick has the unfortunate knack of being in the wrong place at precisely the wrong time.'

So is Nick Faldo misunderstood? It is more likely that he is not understood well enough since he has distanced himself deliberately from the mainstream of Tour life in his quest for success. Now he has achieved it and also become a devoted father to his new family, there are signs that a closer relationship between Faldo and the public is very much on the cards.

NICK FALDO

Nicknamed 'The Dog' for his terrier-like adherence to his principles, David Graham is what a soccer manager might refer to as a 'hard man'. Getting his retaliation in first is perhaps too harsh an assessment of the lean Australian approach, but Graham certainly presents a somewhat abrasive front to the world.

Raised in poverty and from a broken home, Graham's early life was one of hardship, but relief from these pressures could be found at the local golf course near his home in Windsor, New South Wales. His first clubs were an old set of left-handed models and it speaks volumes for his determination that he became a competent player with these before switching to playing right-handed. He determined to become a professional golfer, a decision that did not meet with approval from his father who threatened to disown him if he took that step before he had finished his education. The irresistible force of Graham's desire against the immoveable object of his father's wishes caused an irrevocable split. Still the hammer blows rained down on his psyche. His first job as a club professional ended in failure and bankruptcy and he worked in a golf club factory to pay off his creditors.

He embarked on the tournament trail having developed a somewhat rigid, mechanical swing and a painstaking study of each shot. His first international success occurred in the 1970 French Open but he really caught the public eye when, in the same year in partnership with Bruce Devlin, he helped Australia to victory in the World Cup. Further victories in the Far East followed before he decided to commit himself totally to the US Tour. His first victory came in 1972 when he defeated Devlin in a play-off but thereafter other titles were hard to come by.

The problem was that Graham had little incentive to win money and tournaments, for at the beginning of his professional career he had entered into a rash agreement with a manager who was bleeding him for virtually every dollar he earned. It wasn't until he won his second tournament in 1976 that he was able to buy out his contract and build his career on a sound financial footing.

Life took on a rosier hue when he won again in America that year and then took the World Match-Play Championship with a stunning display of putting in the final against Hale Irwin. The man with the methodical method then broke through to win the 1979 US PGA Championship after a play-off with Ben Crenshaw, took Nicklaus's Memorial Tournament in 1980 by holing from 30 feet on the final green and the scaled new heights in the 1981 US Open at Merion. His final round of 67 to win by one stroke is regarded as perhaps the finest finishing round in modern times in terms of sheer consistency. He missed just one fairway and hit all 18 greens in regulation figures.

It was the pinnacle of a career that had been established against all odds and it is hardly surprising that events have left their mark on his character. Now approaching his mid-40s, Graham has mellowed with the passing years. He has two teenage sons and whenever he is at home takes them to see the Dallas Cowboys football team who are his abiding passion. His other interests include hunting, cars and golf club design, the latter subject being one at which he is an acknowledged expert, at one time designing clubs for Jack Nicklaus.

DAVID GRAHAM

Bank managers and bank staff in general are not noted for their carefree flamboyance. The business of dealing with other people's money breeds an innate sense of caution, leaving little room for creative flights of fancy.

After seven years as a bank teller, during which time he won the New Zealand Open as an amateur, Bob Charles turned professional and brought a banker's logic to golf. So far as Charles was concerned, the bottom line hinged on getting the ball in the hole with the putter. The rest of the game was merely a preliminary exercise and so he trained himself to avoid errors through the green and, once on the putting surface, really got down to business.

Charles was introduced to golf at the age of five by his parents who were both keen performers. They were also left-handers and since their clubs were easily available, it was a matter of convenience that their son should use them. In fact, Charles was naturally ambidextrous, using the right hand for one-handed operations such as writing and bowling at cricket and reversing to left-handed for two-handed games such as batting and playing golf.

Having turned professional in 1960, Charles won the New Zealand professional title in 1961 and then re-wrote the record books in 1963. Until that time no New Zealander, let alone a left-handed New Zealander, had ever come close to winning a major championship. In the Open Championship of that year at Royal Lytham & St Annes he averaged 30 putts per round and his total of 277 tied with the American, Phil Rodgers. In the 36-hole play-off, the Charles putting stroke was absolutely devastating and with 26 putts in the morning round and 31 in the afternoon he buried poor Rodgers by eight strokes.

Although he came close to the Open title on a couple of other occasions, he never won another major but continued to compile a fair record in all parts of the world. His victory in the 1969 World Match-Play Championship was another example of his sorcery on the greens when, in the final against Gene Littler, he holed from 30 feet on the final green to send the match into extra holes before winning. He was a fine bad-weather player when his policy of keeping the ball in play and then holing out ruthlessly paid extra dividends.

Charles married a South African girl and for some time lived in that country but now lives most of the time in America where he has discovered a new lease of life on the US Senior Tour. In 1988 he topped the Senior Tour money list with over $500,000, more money in one year than in his entire career in Europe.

Watching the Charles swing and the famed putting stroke was like watching a right-hander in a mirror; moreover, it was a mirrored right-hander whose expression never altered. He has always been a somewhat dour, taciturn performer whose post-round comments are restricted to how the numbers on the score-card were achieved. He enjoys playing table-tennis, watching cricket and rearing sheep on his farm in his native land.

BOB CHARLES

The first man to win a million dollars from tournament golf was Arnold Palmer who reached that milestone in 1968 after 13 years as a professional. In 1988, Curtis Strange won over a million dollars in a single season on the US Tour, thus demonstrating not only the inflationary times in which we live but also the futility of using money-winnings as a yardstick of achievement. Not even Strange himself would begin to compare his record with that of Palmer's, but as his career has developed so has his name become more linked to that of his illustrious predecessor.

Indirectly, it was Palmer who fired Strange's desire to become a touring professional. Watching P almer's exploits on television during the 1960s gave Strange the impetus. Not that he was a stranger to golf, his father was the professional and owner of the White Sands Country Club in Virginia Beach, Virginia. Both Curtis and his twin brother Allan, the elder by 60 seconds, spent their childhood years between the golf course and the baseball diamond. At the age of 12, young Curtis made the big decision and gave up baseball where he was a promising pitcher and catcher. Two years later his father died so his game came under the scrutiny of Chandler Harper, the former US PGA champion.

The Palmer influence cropped up again when Strange went to Wake Forest, Palmer's old college, on a Palmer sports scholarship. Major amateur honours followed as well as a place in the 1975 US Walker Cup team which contained such players as Jerry Pate, Craig Stadler, Jay Haas and Gary Koch, all of whom have made their presence felt as professionals.

Strange turned professional in 1976 and was considered one of the certainties for stardom.

Unaccountably, he missed winning his player's card at his first attempt in the qualifying school, confessing later that he just couldn't handle the pressure.

He came on Tour the following year and became an assiduous practiser. His fellow professionals agree that no-one works harder at his game than Strange and no-one is tougher. In his early professional years he gained the reputation of being too tough for his own good. He was too hard on himself on the course and, when things went wrong, a quick temper came to the surface. Enter Palmer again. In the 1982 Bay Hill Classic, which is Palmer's own tournament in Florida, Strange blew up on the course and his temper got the better of him. Palmer gave him a public remonstration.

Since the 1985 US Masters, which he nearly won after a first-round 80, Strange has become the major money-winner on the US Tour. Three times in four years he has led the money list and was regarded as the main hope to restore some of the fading pride in American golf. He took a major step in that direction when he won the 1988 US Open after a play-off with Nick Faldo, but as a truly international player there are still a number of question marks. In 1985 he by-passed the Open Championship at Royal St George's but two weeks later pitched up for the Dutch Open which guaranteed him a fat appearance fee, not the best way to build an enduring record.

At home with his wife, Sarah, and their two sons Strange is really a good old Southern boy who likes nothing better than going off with his pals for some huntin', shootin' and fishin'. It's his way of relaxing away from a Tour where money records are easily broken but, as Curtis Strange realises only too well, tournament victories are something which can never be taken away.

CURTIS STRANGE

In the post-war chaos that was Europe in 1945, thousands of refugees were transported to Russia never to be heard of again. It was on one of these trains that Erwin Langer, a Czech from the Sudetenland, found himself in September of that year.

When Hitler had annexed his country in 1938, Langer, a farmer, had been forced to join the German Army and now, as one of a defeated nation, he was being taken to an unknown destination deep in the USSR. Fortunately, the train was poorly guarded and a few miles short of the border, Langer was able to jump the train and escape. Eight months and several hundred miles later he was reunited with his parents in the town of Augsburg, near Munich, and was able to start a new life as a bricklayer.

This determination to overcome all odds has been passed on to Bernhard Langer, Erwin's second son. Very few current players of world stature have worked as hard on their game as the fair-haired Bavarian and none of them has had to fight such a protracted battle with the golfer's dread disease, the 'yips'. Yet, as a teenager he had been an outstanding putter whose chief failings were a tendency to wildness in the longer shots. He took his first swings at the age of nine when his elder brother took him down to the local course near their home. Some of the members provided him with some old unmatched clubs and, as he grew, he developed a very strong long game.

He first emerged in Europe in 1976 at the age of 18 and found the experience somewhat overwhelming. A reserved and rather shy young man, he was alone without any German-speaking colleagues and competing against the likes of Jacklin and Ballesteros. Quite simply, his nerve cracked. From being an instinctive putter, he became one of the saddest cases of the 'yips' the game has ever seen. The first time his affliction became public was when he was selected to play for the Continent against Britain. It was a nightmare. He missed every short putt in sight. He was so pathetic on the greens that spectators turned away with embarrassment, concerned that they too would succumb to the infection.

It was, perhaps, a relief for Langer when he had to leave golf for eighteen months while he served in the army. On his return to civilian life he was a more assured individual and set to work to eliminate his putting problems. Hour after hour was spent working on an effective stroke until one began to evolve. The acquisition of a new putter in 1980 was the final piece in the rehabilitation process. Langer started to win tournaments. His confidence swelled and his long game took on an awesome aspect. Occasionally, the parasite in his system would emerge to frolic with his psyche as it did in the 1982 PGA Championship at Hillside when he four-putted the 16th green in the final round. On paper, however, Langer stood as a shining example of a man who had conquered the 'yips' through sheer application and Teutonic thoroughness.

He became an international figure after his US Masters victory in 1985 but still found it difficult to assert his personality. He is quiet, modest and unassuming. His remark that he found Severiano Ballesteros 'intimidating' after their final in the 1984 World Match-Play was widely interpreted as part of a long-term feud between the two. In fact, it was no more than the comment of a sensitive man on the Spaniard's dark, and sometimes brooding, countenance.

Deeply religious but not to the point of being evangelical, Bernhard Langer is a man who keeps golf in perspective. It is a game which has brought him untold wealth and, considering his background, his country of birth and his putting woes, his achievements are quite remarkable. Maybe his putting will gradually force him out of the very top rank but his interest in developing the game in Germany and the construction of new courses there mean that his contribution will be lasting.

BERNHARD LANGER

To a certain extent, Rodger Davis fits in perfectly with everyone's idea of a typical Aussie. Open and friendly and everybody's mate, Davis likes to chew the fat over a game of cards and a few beers and is a keen follower of all sports.

Behind that cheerful exterior lurks a sharp golfing brain which is now beginning to reap rewards that a few years ago looked extremely remote. Indeed, life couldn't be much sweeter for the man whose trademark is the colourful plus twos and matching hose with his name embroidered on them, but who, a few years ago, was facing not only the destruction of his career but also financial ruin.

Born in Sydney, Davis's introduction to golf started when he caddied for the professional at the Gordon Club near his home. Something of a boy prodigy, he became captain of the New South Wales State junior team and won every junior title available before turning professional in 1974. His first victories came in 1977 in Australia and it was in that year that he made his first foray onto the European Tour.

Two years later his name was very much to the forefront, first when he led the English Classic at The Belfry after two rounds but then fell away dramatically, and second when he led the Open Championship at Royal Lytham with just five holes to play, an ugly double-bogey at the 14th putting paid to his hopes. Again in 1980 he led in The Belfry tournament after two rounds before collapsing again and inevitably the question marks arose concerning his ability to take the pressure. But Davis was made of sterner stuff and in 1981 he finally gained his revenge on that particular course by taking the State Express Classic for his first European title.

It was during the following year that the rot began to set in. Davis developed a chronic case of the 'yips', the putting affliction for which there is no known cure. His performances and prize-money slumped and, seeing no relief, he decided to pack up the life of a globe-trotting professional and bought a motel and restaurant on the holiday coast of Queensland. Putting down roots of this nature would also allow him to be with his wife and two children. The motel venture failed and Davis was left with debts of £160,000. There was only one way to recover and that was to get back on the golf course.

The search for solvency provided strong motivation and Davis's efforts since his return in 1984 have subsequently turned him into an international player of some repute. In 1986 he won the PGA Championship at Wentworth and helped Australia win the Dunhill Cup, and in one season wiped out that dent with winnings of over £180,000. He matched that figure in 1987 and in that year finished one stroke behind Nick Faldo in the Open Championship after equalling the Muirfield course record with an opening 64. In 1988 he again exceeded £100,000 in prize-money in Europe, but his financial rehabilitation was completed, appropriately, in his native land. The Bicentennial Classic at Royal Melbourne carried an enormous first prize of £250,000 and it was Davis who won it.

There were a few tears shed then and more than a few 'tinnies' opened. The man with the half-pace swing and the perceptible pause at the top had become an Australian folk hero, a bloke who had battled his way back and shown everyone what Aussie grit and determination are all about.

RODGER DAVIS

Mention the name of Jan Stephenson in male company and there will be a lot of knowing growls of approval and the odd nudge and wink. This is to be expected since she has become the sex symbol of the US LPGA Tour, and although she protests that she would rather be known as a player than as a sweater girl in the Lana Turner mould, her numerous provocative poses place the emphasis firmly on the latter.

She first became known in her native land of Australia when she won the New South Wales schoolgirl title six years in a row and followed that with four consecutive wins in the Australian Junior Championship. She felt that as an amateur her future was limited in Australia, particularly as she had upset the establishment by criticising its selection of older players for teams ahead of younger, more talented girls. Turning professional she spent a year in Australia before going to America. She had $4000 stake money and a great deal of determination. The money nearly ran out before she won her first cheque but her performances in that first year won her the Rookie of the Year award for 1974.

Following her first wins in 1976, people began to take more than a little notice of her. Her combination of stunning looks and an aggressive game seemed a perfect combination to promote the fortunes of the Tour. But Stephenson had problems of her own adjusting to her new environment. Her relationships with the other players were not exactly harmonious and she was considered aloof and arrogant. It was apparent that some of the American players resented her success and also her glamorous image.

Further victories followed and then Stephenson really blew the lid off the whole affair by appearing in the LPGA's promotional magazine lying on a bed in a revealing white dress. A chorus of disapproval greeted this with some of the other players referring to the picture as 'quasi-pornographic'. The LPGA, though, received a wave of publicity, galleries swelled and prize-money grew. Stephenson couldn't complain either because the pose preluded her best year on Tour at that time.

She declined offers to pose from both *Playboy* and *Penthouse*, feeling their approaches were not in the best of taste, but she was unashamed about using her undoubted physical assets. 'Just because we're athletes,' she once said, 'doesn't mean we have to look like truck-drivers. I'm as feminine as they come and proud of it.' Her next LPGA picture saw her as Marilyn Monroe in the classic pavement pose from 'The Seven Year Itch' and she has continued her pulchritudinous ways with a series of calendars in which she is depicted as having a bath wearing nothing but several hundred golf balls. Her career peaked in 1983 when she won the US Women's Open and although she has been a steady money winner since, she is one of the few women golfers to have contracted the 'yips' on the greens. An extremely hard worker, she drove herself relentlessly to become the best in the world but complications in her personal life have tended to divert her. She has a full, free, uninhibited swing which creates a follow-through position that anyone over the age of 30 would be unwise to try and emulate. She stands as the game's true sex goddess, the epitome of the expression 'If you've got it, flaunt it.' Flaunt it she did and the world of women's professional golf should be eternally grateful.

JAN STEPHENSON

'Some golfers are born to disaster, some achieve disaster and some have disaster thrust upon them.' It is unlikely that Tsuneyuki Nakajima is a student of Shakespeare and even less likely that he is in the habit of bowdlerising the Bard and his works. However, it must be said that in modern professional tournament golf no other player has built up such an accident-prone reputation than the stocky bespectacled player from Japan.

Nakajima started to play at the age of nine under the guidance of his father. Since the family was not wealthy enough to play on a course, much of the tuition took place in the small back garden of the family home. Nonetheless, the instruction was thorough. Nakajima senior would tell his son to put on waterproofs and then, while he hit balls into a net, the father would turn the hose on him, and blast him with a huge electric fan to simulate various weather conditions.

The reward for this application was victory in the Japanese Amateur Championship at the age of 18. He was the youngest winner of the title and a golden career in the professional ranks beckoned. His victory in the 1977 Japan PGA provided him with the opportunity to make his name in the international arena as he was invited to play in the US Masters at Augusta the following April. Unfortunately, the way he made his name was not one he would have chosen.

Playing the 13th he hooked his tee shot into the creek which meanders up the hole before crossing in front of the green. He dropped out under penalty and hit his third shot up the fairway. His pitch to the green fell into the creek but he felt he could play the ball. He played it quite well but the ball bounced back off the bank and hit him on the foot, thereby adding two penalty strokes. He handed the club back to his caddie who dropped it in the water – two more penalty strokes were added to the ledger. Finally, Nakajima pitched over the green with his tenth shot, chipped and two-putted for a 13.

The Japanese are a philosophical nation and Nakajima believed that the gods would compensate him for his woes at some future date. But the golfing gods are perverse and in July of the same year, while playing in the Open Championship at St Andrews, Nakajima was struck again on the infamous Road Hole. Here he was on the front of the green in two shots, putted up the crest and watched in anguish as the ball turned sharp left into the Road Bunker. Four attempts later he regained the green and walked off with a nine.

A rather shy and diffident young man, Nakajima retreated back to his native land after these traumas and set about rebuilding his shattered confidence. He emerged three years later a much more solid player and began to make an impact. His appearances among the leaders became more frequent and he was christened 'Tommy' by an Australian television commentator who couldn't get his tongue round Tsuneyuki. In 1983 he won nine times in Japan and emerged as the natural successor to Isao Aoki as Japan's leading player being four times leader of the Japanese Order of Merit.

Highly successful at home, he has yet to win an important title elsewhere. In the 1986 Open Championship at Turnberry he lay one stroke behind the leader after three rounds but fell away in the final round. In the 1987 US Open he again challenged for the lead in the third round before the old disaster jinx grabbed him again when he lost a ball up a tree on the final hole.

For all his toubles, Tommy Nakajima retains a quiet, self-deprecating sense of humour which has endeared him to his fellow professionals. Perhaps his attitude can best be illustrated by an incident which occurred when he was partnering Joey Sindelar in a four-ball better-ball tournament in America. On one hole, Nakajima's ball landed squarely behind a tree. Sindelar came across and made sympathetic noises such as 'Gee, that's a tough break, Tommy.' Nakajima looked at him with an air of a man who has been through it all. 'No big deal, Joey,' he said, 'no big deal.'

TOMMY NAKAJIMA

If all the eccentricities of great Irish golfers were put into one swing it would probably turn out like Eamonn Darcy's. There's a trace of James Bruen's famous loop in the takeaway, a hint of Christy O'Connor's wristiness at the top and a little of Harry Bradshaw's scythe-like action through the ball. The net result of this combination is one of the oddest swings in the professional game; in one vital area, however, the twelve inches either side of the ball, Darcy is totally orthodox.

A native of Delgany, near Dublin, young Eamonn harboured boyhood dreams of becoming a jockey but he soon grew too big for that and took to golf. The theory behind the origins of the Darcy swing is that the Delgany course is built round the perimeter of a large hill with all the holes running in an anti-clockwise direction. Thus, if the club were swung in normal fashion it would simply bang against the hill behind the player, therefore it had to be picked up sharply. Pure Irish whimsy of course, but it's an explanation that couldn't come from any other part of the world.

Controlling all those moving parts in the swing requires a great sense of timing and a feel for the clubhead. These attributes have provided Darcy with one of the best short games in Europe and he is a magician with those little shots round the green which he executes with an old ladies' wedge which was probably used by a very old lady, such is its antiquity.

Darcy turned professional in 1969 but scavenged in the lower reaches of the Tour until 1974 when he finished 36th in the rankings. The following year he catapulted himself into the limelight when he led the field after three rounds in the PGA Championship at Royal St George's. Moreover, he was ahead of Arnold Palmer who had been specially imported for the event. Could the man with the shinty swing stand up to Palmer and the onslaught of a howling gale which swept the course on the final day? The answer, sadly, was no but he stood up well enough to take second place behind the great American. The following year, in the same tournament over the same course, he finished in a tie for first place with Gary Player and Neil Coles before succumbing to the Englishman at the third extra hole. His first victory came in that year when he won the Under-25s title and in partnership with Christy O'Connor Junior took the old Sumrie Four-Ball event.

Tournament victories have been a little thin on the ground for Darcy, he has only three major titles to his name in Europe and maybe that swing has not provided as much consistency as its owner would have liked. For all that, Eamonn Darcy's name is carved indelibly in the annals of European golf for one shot he hit in the 1987 Ryder Cup match at Muirfield Village. Playing against Ben Crenshaw, who was putting with a one-iron having shattered his putter, Darcy went from three up to one down with two to play. He squared the match with a birdie on the 17th and on a tension-filled final day, then faced a downhill putt of five feet on the last green to secure another vital European point. He holed it and in one moment redeemed an otherwise moderate Ryder Cup record.

Another supreme moment, this time in the history of Irish golf, came when Darcy captained his team of Des Smyth and Ronan Rafferty to victory in the 1988 Dunhill Cup. His philosophy as captain was quite simple: 'I just tell them what they have to do and they go off and do what they like.'

With his quirky swing, his ruddy complexion and his carroty-red hair, Eamonn Darcy is the archetypal Irishman. Like all Irishmen he likes a good 'crack', a yarn or two over a few jars of the dark stuff and like most of his countrymen he has a keen appreciation of horseflesh, whether the animals are carrying him or merely his money.

EAMONN DARCY

In the early 1960s the media hype caught on quickly to the concept of golf's Big Three, Arnold Palmer, Gary Player and Jack Nicklaus. All were, at that time, manaed by Mark McCormack and the title was indeed an effective marketing weapon. In terms of golfing ability, however, it should have been the Big Four because William Earl Casper was undoubtedly one of the great players of that era.

Casper was not managed by McCormack but even if he had been it is doubtful whether he would have altered his low-profile, and he certainly wouldn't have altered his approach to the game. In the blood and thunder of the halycon Palmer years, Casper was quietly efficient. His drives never boomed from the tee, his irons never fizzed around the hole – but, boy, could he putt. He realised that putting represented fifty per cent of the game and set out to maximise that potential.

The Casper putting stroke was not from the stiff-armed pendulum school favoured by that other supreme putter, Bob Charles; instead Casper broke his wrists on the backswing and then popped the ball forward with the right-hand. It was highly unorthodox but how well it worked. When he won his first US Open at Winged Foot in 1959 he took just 112 putts for the four rounds, a total which caused Ben Hogan to comment: 'If you couldn't putt you'd be selling hot dogs outside the ropes.'

Casper's brand of conservative golf fitted his conservative character. While others strutted the fairways in a multitude of peacock hues, he stuck with the drab colours of late autumn. His record of winning at least one tournament every year between 1956 and 1971 brought him admiration but not adulation. In an effort to boost his saleability he took on a manager who was more used to handling show-business stars than sports stars. This was Ed Barner, who was later to handle Severiano Ballesteros on Casper's recommendation, and it was Barner who conceived the idea of marketing Casper's allergies. It was discovered that Casper was allergic to, of all things, grass and the only thing which helped was a diet of buffalo steaks. The hyping of 'Buffalo Bill' the golfer was not a resounding success but Casper still follows a strict diet and lists nutrition as one of his major interests.

Of course, the American public never really forgave Casper for what he did to Arnold Palmer in the 1966 US Open when Casper made up a seven-stroke deficit over the final nine holes to earn a tie and then win the play-off. The two represented both ends of the golfing spectrum – Palmer the swashbuckling hero, Casper the methodical plodder.

Golf was never the consuming passion in Casper's life. His priorities lay with his family; he and his wife Shirley had eleven children, six of whom were adopted, and he was a devout Mormon. He won over $1.5 million in his career on the US Tour and gave a percentage of it to the Mormon church. Towards the end of his full-time playing career he made a disastrous investment in peach farming and lost most of his fortune. His game also suffered disastrously but he pieced it back together again and was able to earn another fortune on the US Senior Tour where he cuts a bizarre figure wearing a series of flamboyant outfits in direct contrast to those he wore in his prime.

BILLY CASPER

The first black American professional to make any impact on the game was Charlie Sifford who was probably better known for the fat Havana cigars he continually chomped on while playing. Sifford was the first of his race to win a US Tour event, the 1967 Greater Hartford Open, and he also won the 1969 Los Angeles Open. Neither of these victories earned him a place in the US Masters and the rumblings of discontent regarding Southern prejudice were not silenced until Lee Elder made the breakthrough in 1975.

The US Tour, however, had been fully integrated for some time. Prior to that, black professionals had their own circuit, the United Golf Association Tour which offered minimal prize-money and was known disparagingly as the 'peanut circuit'.

The American country club scene remains a WASP-dominated arena and the opportunities for young black children to progress in golf are few. All of which makes the story of Calvin Peete one of the most remarkable in modern sports.

Peete was born in Detroit, the youngest of nine children. His parents separated and he went to live with his father, a migrant farm-worker who had re-married, and young Calvin thus became the eldest of eleven half-brothers and sisters. Working the fields in Florida alongside his father, Peete felt that life had more to offer than plucking vegetables from the ground. He obtained a peddler's licence at the age of 17, bought an old station-wagon and joined the migrant workers on their trek up the East Coast selling jewelry and trinkets. Some of the places he visited were not noted for their sobriety or high moral tone but Peete plied his wares wherever he could and even had two diamonds implanted in his front teeth to add shine to his sales pitch.

His travels took him to Rochester, New York where he had some friends. The friends were keen golfers and would invariably ask Peete to join them. At first Peete thought the game was a futile pastime, besides which he had a permanently bent left arm, the result of a childhood accident when he fell out of a tree. Then he saw a televised tournament which informed him that Jack Nicklaus was making $200,000 a year from golf; in 1966, Peete felt he could live off one-third of that so gave the game a try.

Long hours of practice taught him that with his disability he would never be a power hitter so he worked to develop a rhythm which would produce accuracy. He struggled at first to get onto the US Tour but made the important breakthrough in 1979 when he won his first tournament. From then on the virtues of hard work that had so shaped his early life paid off. He became the most relentlessly straight hitter in the modern game and the tournament victories, and the money, flowed his way.

Pressure is always relative and Peete's background made living a pressurised situation; compared with that, pressure in golf seemed like a bed of roses. He realises that he acts as an example to others of his race and that he can influence the young and perhaps help them follow his path. Aware of these responsibilities he had the diamonds removed from his teeth because he wanted to be recognised for his qualities as a golfer rather than the guy who flashed a big smile. He was asked once what golf really meant to him, to which he replied: 'It sure as hell beats selling jewelry in a cat-house in New Orleans.' Then he smiled, and, even without the diamonds, his smile still sparkled.

CALVIN PEETE

Mark McNulty is what might be termed a 'neat' golfer. From the tip of his shoes to the top of the white cap that is his trademark, nothing is out of place. There are a few flamboyant touches about McNulty, unless you count the pencil moustache which gives him the air of a Mississippi gambler, and he is not the kind of player who excites the galleries with feats of derring-do. His game from tee to green is quietly efficient, not spectacularly powerful but long enough; once in the vicinity of the green, however, a new McNulty appears, a deadly marksman with wedge and putter who is known as 'McMagic'.

Born in Bindura, Zimbabwe of farming parents, McNulty grew up in the tiny district of Centenary. His father was killed in a shooting accident when his son was only 14 months old. By the time he was three he was following his mother round the Centenary course and taking the odd swipe at a ball. When he was nine he was taken to Salisbury to see a challenge match between Gary Player and Arnold Palmer and his first view of Palmer was enough to determine his future. From then on, other sports took second place in his total commitment to golf and by the time he was 16 he was a scratch player. Even when he left school and had to serve the mandatory stint in the army, allowances were made for his golfing talent and he eventually embarked on a professional career.

His first forays into Europe were pretty successful and he broke through to win in only his second year, 1979. Another victory followed in 1980 and life seemed set fair as the money rolled in and McNulty was able to indulge his passion for fast cars.

It was a passion which nearly cost him his life when, setting off one day from his home to travel to Europe, he suddenly realised he had left a suitcase behind. He jumped out to check the boot and make sure, then got back in, forgetting to put on his seat belt. Moments later a bus hit him head-on, but apart from a broken nose and other facial injuries, the accident left no permanent damage.

He then tried his luck in America but like so many before him, it became the graveyard of his confidence and his swing gradually deteriorated. Then he had to have a cartilage operation on his knee which became septic and when he eventually got back on the course, his game was in tatters.

While he was competing in junior events in Zimbabwe, McNulty had become firm friends with Nick Price and a man called David Leadbetter. Price and McNulty loved to play but Leadbetter was the studious one, more likely to be reading a book or magazine article on the theory of the game than actually playing. It was to Leadbetter that McNulty turned as his fellow-countryman was now an established 'guru' on the game and operating from a course in Florida. Leadbetter told McNulty that his swing had to be rebuilt from scratch, most notably the grip and the plane of the swing. It took a great deal of sweat and effort but McNulty mastered it and became one of the most consistent players on the European scene.

His long game is renowned for its steadiness and, of course, the magical short game is as masterly as ever. Perhaps this is not so surprising for a man whose touch round the greens is reflected in his ability to play the piano in an accomplished manner and who lists snooker as his favourite relaxation. The love of fast cars has been replaced by a desire for luxury cars and his prize-money in recent years has enabled him to indulge that desire to the full. Quietly confident and determined, Mark McNulty may never contend for an Open Championship title simply because he lacks the fire-power, but week in, week out on the Tour he's the best each-way bet around.

MARK McNULTY

Watching Ray Floyd on the practice ground alongside his fellow professionals, the casual observer would pause only briefly before moving along to absorb something more elegant. The Floyd swing is no thing of beauty. It looks laboured, jerky and in possession of a multitude of moving parts, not least a pronounced loop at the top. However, when you are well over six feet tall, solidly built but with disproportionately short arms, then you have to make certain adjustments in order to strike a golf ball effectively.

Floyd has been making these adjustments consistently since he first came on the US Tour in 1963 and, at the age of 20 years five months, became the third youngest winner of all time on the Tour. That first victory did not, however, herald a string of wins, chiefly because Floyd was having too good a time with extra-curricular activities. His two closest companions at that time were Doug Sanders and Al Besselink, two players who were notorious for their dedication to enjoyment of wine and women and who took it upon themselves to educate the young Floyd in the finer points of their interests. Floyd became a willing pupil, keeping wild hours, arriving on the first tee sometimes without having had any sleep. When asked the colour of his eyes he replied: 'Usually pretty red.' He also held the unusual distinction of being the only golf professional who had a share in a topless female band.

Marriage and maturity put an end to Floyd's roistering and he broke through to win his first major championship by taking the 1969 US PGA title. This victory was somewhat marred by the fact that Floyd's closest pursuers, Gary Player and to a lesser extent Jack Nicklaus, were victims of anti-apartheid demonstrators during the final round. There was no such question over Floyd's second major victory. This was the 1976 US Masters which he won in a canter having decided to base his attack on Augusta's par-five holes by using a five-wood for his second shots to give the ball a higher trajectory into the green. The plan was a stunning success as Floyd tied Nicklaus's record aggreg ate en route to a nine-stroke win.

He had now developed into one of the toughest players on the Tour with a growing reputation for being the ultimate professional. As his victories and money-winnings grew with each passing year, that reputation was enhanced. Two more major championships came his way, the 1982 US PGA Championship and then, at the age of 43, he became the oldest winner of the US Open when he won in 1986.

Floyd's career therefore provides the golfing parallel to that of the belief that the most rabid Communist undergraduates eventually make the best Conservative politicians. He is reluctant to discuss his early days on Tour which is not surprising for a respected US Ryder Cup captain.

They don't come much tougher on the golf course than Raymond Floyd, and his fellow professionals tend to steer clear of him if he wants to play a practice round for money. He has a sharp temper, particularly if he feels he has been wronged without justification and has had the odd run-in with British crowds when he feels they have cheered inappropriately. Not a player the galleries warm to, he is one they respect for his achievements, despite that rather ungainly swing.

RAY FLOYD

PUNDITS AND GURUS

Just as Arnold Palmer could be regarded as the founder of modern American professional golf, so Tony Jacklin could be regarded as the British version. Jacklin was the pioneer, the man who took on the world, or more specifically America, and made British g olf proud. He was brash, cocky and confident and exciting to watch. If Jacklin had been born an American he might well have been swamped by the number of golfers with a similar approach. As a Briton, however, he stood out like a tree on a links course.

The son of a lorry driver from Scunthorpe, Jacklin's beginnings were humble but his father did play golf and encouraged the youngster to do the same. It soon became apparent that Jacklin Junior had a talent for the game and was intent on making it his profession. He took that plunge in 1962 and quickly upset the establishment with his colourful clothes and his disregard for hidebound traditions. He was still a very young man of course but he knew where he wanted to go.

He arrived there extremely quickly. He won in South Africa and New Zealand and then in 1967 smashed the course record for Royal St George's with a 64 in winning the Dunlop Masters, a round which contained the first televised hole-in-one. He played the US Tour and in 1968 won the Greater Jacksonville Open and now was being hotly tipped to be the first British golfer to break the 18-year spell of overseas domination in the Open Championship.

Most British golfers who are forced to carry the weight of the nation's hopes on their shoulders find it an intolerable burden. Jacklin was the exception. He revelled in it. He knew he had the shots, all he needed was the mood and the inspiration. It came to him in 1969 at Royal Lytham & St Annes when he displayed cool courage to win the Open and fulfil everyone's expectations. The boost to the British game was galvanic and it is not coincidental that the Ryder Cup match of that year ended in a tie.

The mood was still upon Jacklin in 1970. He shook American golf to its very roots by taking the US Open by seven shots and, on returning for the Open at St Andrews, was on a crest. His first nine holes in that Championship were completed in 29 strokes and he had birdied the 10th when fate stepped in with a massive cloudburst which postponed play until the next day. On his return, the mood had deserted Jacklin and it could be said that, from that moment, luck was rarely at his side. It certainly kicked him in the solar plexus in the 1972 Open at Muirfield when Lee Trevino pulled off some quite outrageous flukes to take a title Jacklin had virtually sewn up.

Jacklin was never quite the same player after that and the demands of a now-burgeoning European Tour found him more often the big fish in the small pond. He became John Jacobs's trump card in the building of a cohesive European circuit and could be assured of large appearance fees, something he couldn't receive in America.

The motivation gradually drifted, the striking lost its edge and the putting became the source of all blame. In truth, it was probably more than that – travelling around hitting a golf ball simply wasn't much fun anymore, and then having to justify why you weren't hitting a golf ball quite as well as you should made it all the more tedious. Jacklin never had the dedication of a Gary Player or the desire of a Jack Nicklaus, he played golf on his emotions and was therefore subject to greater disparity between the peaks and troughs. Yet it is this emotional reaction that has made Jacklin the most successful Ryder Cup captain from this side of the Atlantic, for he was able to weld a team of several nationalities into a single unit with a common will to win. Other British players have now overtaken Jacklin's achievements in global terms but this cannot detract from the fact that he was the first to take on the world and give it a run for its money.

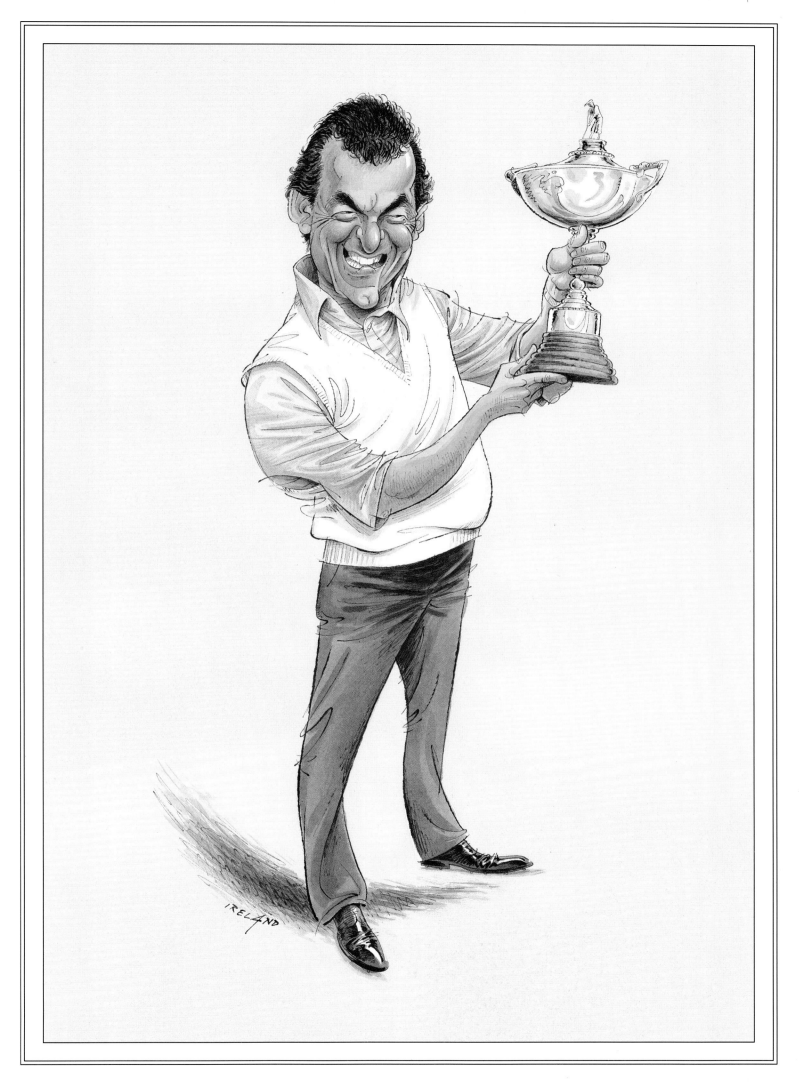

TONY JACKLIN

'So many people are afraid to admit they are trying – I am not.' Thus, in his own words, did Henry Cotton sum up his attitude to competing at his chosen profession in an age when such an approach was considered as not quite 'playing the game'.

Educated at a public school – Alleyn's in Dulwich – he broke the tradition that professionals should be horny-handed sons of toil, doffing their caps regularly at the gentry of club membership. His background equipped him with a broader view of the possibilities of success as a professional golfer, and when he turned professional at the age of 16, in 1923, he pursued his career with a rare single-mindedness and dedication.

Realising that the great players of the day were in America, Cotton took off to the United States in 1928 to learn what lay at the source of their domination. This was the era of Hagen and Jones, who monopolised the Open Championship. He returned six months later, having recovered most of the £350 the trip cost him, and, more importantly, had learned to draw the ball for greater length. This was a crucial step in his development and from then on he became the finest striker of the ball Britain had seen since the days of Vardon. The repetitiveness of his swing, allied to intense concentration, made him a formidable competitor, and, having made his debut in the 1929 Ryder Cup when he won the decisive single in a British victory, he then set about achieving his ambition of winning the Open Championship.

The Open was the one event which motivated him above all others and he geared his life from year to year to winning it. He achieved his goal in 1934 at Royal St George's, his second round of 65 being the score that was to be emblazoned on millions of Dunlop balls thereafter. Hailed as the saviour of British golf, Cotton's victory inspired an unbroken run of British winners up to the war. Not least among these was his second win in 1937 at Carnoustie, his final round of 71 in relentless rain being regarded as one of the finest ever played in the Championship.

There is little doubt that but for the war he would have won more Opens. However, one more victory was to come his way, at Muirfield in 1948. The highlight of this victory was a second round of 66, a round fit for a king, *and* witnessed by one, namely George VI. Now aged 41 and beginning to feel the effects of ill-health, he began to curtail his tournament appearances and his last win came in 1954 when he was 47.

Throughout his career, Cotton was always his own man. He believed that the skills he had worked so hard to hone deserved their due reward and that the public would be willing to pay for the best. He made himself a 'star' in the truest sense of the word, even, at one time, topping the bill at the London Coliseum with a demonstration of his swing. Inevitably, his demands that the petty rules which applied to professionals should not apply to him led him into conflict with authority but he never wavered and, by so doing, gave his profession the respect it now enjoys.

He himself enjoyed the best of life and at one time had a suite at Claridges and a house in Belgravia. He was comfortable in the millionaire playgrounds of Europe and projected the image of the sleek-haired matinée idol. He knew that the press would hang on his every word and shamelessly cultivated relationships with them while they, equally shamelessly, allowed themselves to be cultivated.

He was a lucid speaker, fluent in French, Spanish and Portuguese (and a recounter of risqué jokes in all three languages plus English), writer of several books and a fine teacher. His own thoughts on the golf swing were always focused on the hands – 'a golfer is only as good as his hands, my boy' was his inevitable response to questions on technique. He was an innovator, architect and campaigner for the emancipation of the British golf professional. Young hopefuls flocked to his villa in Portugal's Penina Hotel complex, the course he designed and where he lived for the greater part of his later life. Knighted for his services to the game, he died before he could receive the accolade but his legacy is evident in the status now enjoyed by those who play the game for a living.

HENRY COTTON

Urbane, worldly and immediately identifiable, Peter Alliss is the definitive 'Voice of Golf', the man whose mellifluous tones drift through the drawing-rooms of the nation whenever golf is televised.

Such is the power of the medium that Alliss is now instantly recognisable even to those people who have only a passing interest in the game and yet, nearly 20 years after he retired from serious competitive play, few remember his outstanding ability.

Peter Alliss was born, if not with a silver spoon in his mouth, then certainly within gripping distance of a varnished three-wood. His father, Percy, was among the top half-dozen British professionals in the 1930s, good enough to play in four Ryder Cup matches, win the British Professional Match-Play title a couple of times and narrowly miss out on at least one Open Championship. Percy's Achilles heel was located in his putting stroke and, as fate would have it, the affliction was hereditary.

Hitting a golf ball came naturally and instinctively to young Peter and from an early age he was tipped for stardom. At the age of 22 he was selected for the Ryder Cup match, held that year at Wentworth. It was a baptism of fire as the outcome depended on the matches involving him and the other baby of the team, Bernard Hunt. Inexperience cost both of them the chance to bring glory to Britain and, in Alliss's case, left scars that were a long time healing. He eventually came to terms with that defeat and in subsequent appearances compiled one of the best records, claiming some notable scalps, including that of Arnold Palmer in his prime. He twice won the Vardon Trophy for topping the merit list and in 1958 completed a dazzling run of scoring by winning three Continental titles in a row.

Towards the end of the 1960s the affliction that had overtaken his father on the greens was well and truly embedded and he announced his retirement from international matches after the tied 1969 Ryder Cup match. He intended to continue as a tournament player but he was gradually drawn to other things. Course architecture with David Thomas and an expanding career in broadcasting and writing meant that the classic Alliss swing became increasingly a means for demonstration. Besides, the 'twitch' was by now rampant.

Seated at the feet of the broadcasting master, Henry Longhurst, Alliss soaked up the tricks of the trade and there are those who would say that the pupil copies too closely his predecessor. Certainly there are similarities in the delivery but Alliss has not developed the Churchillian rumble that preceded a Longhurst *bon mot*. He is more likely to produce a schoolboy witticism that, although unsophisticated, is always apposite for the situation.

Peter Alliss always appeared slightly apologetic as a top-class professional golfer, as though he was sorry to have gone round in 66 and won. A lack of ruthlessness, however, is no bad thing if you have a wide-ranging imagination and a mind constantly on the lookout for new ways of approaching problems. He is a professional of the old school, believing that certain standards must be maintained and is not afraid to say so when they lapse. His playing career peaked in a far more relaxed era than can be imagined now and his travelling round Britain playing in Lord Roberts Workshop charity events gave him a priceless insight into what makes ordinary amateur golfers tick.

This, perhaps, is his greatest asset as a commentator, the ability to strike the right note and deliver the remark as though he was sitting next to you in your own clubhouse bar.

PETER ALLISS

Golf is a game of paradox. If we want the ball to fly upwards, we have to hit down; if we want the ball to fly low, we have to hit up; if we aim left, the ball will fly to the right; if we aim right, the ball will fly to the left.

Understanding why these things should be so is generally beyond the grasp of the average weekend golfer. Therefore, he or she is content to live with whatever standard shot they have developed over the years. The slicer will aim further and further left to accommodate the slice and the hooker will aim further and further right to allow for the hook.

It is further evidence of the game's paradoxical nature that its outstanding teacher should tackle golfers' problems by studying the result of a golf shot before studying the swing which produced it.

John Jacobs's laws of ball flight brook no argument. While golfers may deceive themselves as to the quality of their strike, the golf ball never flatters and never lies – its flight reveals all and it is Jacobs who has pioneered this approach to the mutual benefit of himself and the thousands of players who have crossed his path.

Born of golfing stock, his father was the professional at Lindrick Golf Club and Jacobs had golf all around him. His father died when the boy was nine years old and it was his Uncle Jack who took over the post at Lindrick where he remained for over fifty years. Young Maurice, as he was known then, helped out in the shop, ate and drank golf and developed into an accomplished player. Following the war, in which he served with the RAF, he became the assistant professional at South Hallamshire Golf Club. From there he took the unusual step of applying for the post of professional at the Gezira Club in Cairo and getting it. It was a decision which was to affect his life in a major way for not only did it lay the foundations for his teaching, it gave him maturity far beyond his 24 years.

When he returned to Britain three years later in 1952 to take up the reins at Sandy Lodge, he had formulated the principles of the golf swing in his mind and was ready to impart them. His own playing career flourished and he played in the 1955 Ryder Cup match in Palm Springs, winning both foursomes and singles. Such were the demands on his time, however, a decision had to be made between teaching or playing.

Teaching club golfers is not easy but teaching world-class professionals must be a lot worse for in the latter case the fault is hardly discernible. Yet Jacobs has painted on a broad canvass. The principles of ball flight apply across the board and the remedies are applied in a sensible, firm manner. After all, if you're telling Jack Nicklaus what he's doing wrong you have to believe you're right.

A strong personality coupled with some good old-fashioned Yorkshire grit created many conflicts and Jacobs has seen his share of controversy. He was at the centre of the large ball versus small ball argument and his belief that the large ball created better strikers rightly won the day. He was the architect of today's modern PGA European Tour, taking over a ramshackle organisation and, in the face of sometimes bitter opposition, laying the foundations for its current prosperity. He captained two Ryder Cup teams, in 1979 and 1981, and has acted as coach to numerous Walker and Curtis Cup teams as well as developing a career in golf centres and course architecture.

An accomplished fisherman and shot, Jacobs is never happier than when he is in the coverts or the pools and where, apparently, he ranks about plus four handicap in both pastimes. Yet he retains his enthusiasm for golf despite the fact that he must have seen every bad shot the game has to offer. Whatever the ailment, however, the first question to any pupil remains the same: 'What's the ball doing?'

JOHN JACOBS

Although the Mayor of Eastbourne may not agree, his town is best noted for two things. First, as a retirement centre for elderly people which has given rise to the title 'God's waiting-room', and second, as the traditional home of the boys' preparatory school.

It was to one of these latter establishments, the splendidly titled St Cyprians, that Henry Longhurst was sent and his attendance was to shape his life. In those days, just after the Great War, St Cyprians bore a passing resemblance to Dickens's Dotheboys Hall. A regime of cold showers, vile food and regular doses of corporal punishment were regarded as essential to maintain the backbone of the British Empire. But beyond the school's forbidding walls lay the verdant pastures of the Royal Eastbourne Golf Club and it was to these that Henry's gaze was inevitably attracted in the midst of conjugating Latin verbs. Thus began a love affair with the game that was to enchant millions of readers.

He then passed through the system to Charterhouse and finally to Clare College, Cambridge where he captained the golf side. His University golf days enabled him to mix with influential people when the team played various clubs and it was through this Old School Tie network that he was recommended for the job of golf correspondent of *The Sunday Times*.

He developed into a master of his craft and his column on the back page of that newspaper became obligatory reading across the nation. His style was concise and simple and he used golf as a vehicle to expound on many different subjects. He also had an insatiable curiosity and would try anything once. His writing therefore roved over such diverse subjects as bob-sledding down the Cresta Run, stag-hunting, standing for Parliament (and winning) and driving an express steam locomotive, this latter experience being, as he described it, 'like driving a six-cylinder motor-car with the big end gone and two flat tyres'.

Golf allowed him to travel everywhere and he collected a rich fund of stories and anecdotes and with the advent of televised golf he was able to use the more repeatable of them in becoming the definitive voice of golf. His 'brilliant flashes of silence' were a result of knowing when not to speak just as much as knowing when to provide a succinct, pithy comment. His views on golf, and on life, were somewhat reactionary and he made no bones about his politics on certain issues, but he moved freely among dukes and dustmen while admitting a degree of snobbishness in preferring dukes because they were usually more interesting.

In terms of golf writing, Henry's contribution was incalculable. He gave it status and credibility and all of us who have followed in his considerable wake should offer him a silent prayer of thanks. His personal life was marred by tragedy with his son and son-in-law killed in accidents while he himself was stricken dreadfully with illness. Throughout it all he maintained a light tone in his writing, even describing how he had contemplated suicide and revealing that the fortifying whisky had put him to sleep before he could take the tablets.

His autobiography *My Life and Soft Times* stands as a fitting epitaph to a man who took golf as a text and turned it into a philosophy for life. And, as he cheerfully admitted, he also managed the trick of doing it all at somebody else's expense.

HENRY LONGHURST